A Newt in Hard Tarn

*An appreciation of
Alfred Wainwright*

Derek Cockell

Derek Cockell

The Wainwright Society

Published by The Wainwright Society 2023
www.wainwright.org.uk

Copyright © Derek Cockell 2023

Quotations and sketches of A. Wainwright
© The Estate of A. Wainwright 2023

All rights reserved. Without limiting the rights under copyright reserved above, no part of this publication may be reproduced, stored in or introduced into a retrieval system, or transmitted, in any form or by means electronic, mechanical, photocopying, or otherwise, without prior permission in writing from the publisher.

Printed in the EU for Latitude Press, Windermere

ISBN 978-0-9935921-5-7

Contents

	Acknowledgements	iv
	The Wainwright Society	v
	The Wainwright Society and Mountain Rescue	vi
	Foreword	vii
	A Newt in Hard Tarn	vii
	Introduction	ix
1	Wainwright: post-Romantic?	1
2	Romantic Landscapes	7
3	Solitary Walker	21
4	Awakening to Beauty	35
5	Nature's Designs	53
6	Emotional Revelations	75
7	Imagining the Past	87
8	Industrial Landscapes	101
9	True Craftsmen	117
10	Conservationist	131
11	Lament for a lost world?	147
	Bibliography	161

Acknowledgements

Jane King and Annie Sellar (The Estate of A. Wainwright), for their support and permission to use material from the works of A. Wainwright;

John Nicoll, for his early encouragement to write the book;

Richard Holmes, for his inspiring biography of Coleridge that set me on the path of discovery of the Romantic poets and their connections with Wainwright;

Hunter Davies, for the use of his research notes and copies of Wainwright's letters, relating to his definitive biography of Wainwright and book of Wainwright's letters, both generously donated to the Society and now housed in the Kendal Archive Centre;

The Kendal Archive Centre, for providing reproductions of the manuscripts from the Wainwright collection used in the preparation of this book;

Eric Robson OBE, Chairman of The Wainwright Society, for writing the Foreword;

Derry Brabbs, for permission to use the photograph of A. Wainwright;

Richard Else, for permission to use the photograph of A. Wainwright and Eric Robson;

The Management Committee of The Wainwright Society, for their support in publishing the book;

The following Society members:

David Johnson, for keeping me on the literary 'straight and narrow' with his skilful editing of the text;

John Bewick, for his technical advice and guidance in preparing the book for printing and publication;

Andrew Stainthorpe, for his expertise and advice in design matters and for the design of the dust jacket.

The Wainwright Society

The primary aims of The Wainwright Society are to keep alive the fellwalking traditions promoted by Alfred Wainwright through his guidebooks and other publications and to keep faith with his vision of introducing a wider audience to fellwalking and caring for the hills.

The inaugural meeting of the Society was held on 9th November 2002, at Ambleside Youth Hostel. This was followed by a walk to the summit of Dove Crag, using the route described on the first page penned by Wainwright in *The Eastern Fells*, fifty years earlier.

The Society has, over the years, raised many thousands of pounds for causes which it believes Wainwright would have appreciated and supported.

If you would like to know more about the work of The Wainwright Society, visit the website: *www.wainwright.org.uk* or email the Secretary at: *secretary@wainwright.org.uk*

Dove Crag
A Lakeland Sketchbook, No. 73

The Wainwright Society and Mountain Rescue

The Society's main beneficiary during 2023 is the umbrella organisation for Mountain Rescue in the Lake District: *The Lake District Search and Mountain Rescue Association*.

A. Wainwright was listed as a member of the Kendal Mountain Rescue Team during the 1950s.

The nett proceeds of sales of this book, after production costs, will be donated to *The Lake District Search and Mountain Rescue Association*, whose individual members provide a life-saving emergency service to walkers and others in danger on the Lake District fells.

A Society Challenge event, 2009
In aid of the Search and Rescue Dogs Association (SARDA)
Photograph courtesy of Jane Hardy

Foreword
by Eric Robson OBE

It's a pleasure to welcome you to this delightful and important new book by Derek Cockell. Many years in the making, it explores the ideas and places that so influenced the writing of Alfred Wainwright – everything from the Romantic poets to obscure and spectacular corners of the Lakeland landscape.

For anyone wanting to understand what truly inspired AW and what drove him to interpret his favoured places with such skill, this is essential reading.

Eric Robson OBE
Chairman, The Wainwright Society

A. Wainwright and Eric Robson
Filming on the Corpse Road from Swindale to Mardale, May 1985
© *Richard Else*

A Newt in Hard Tarn

'Some of my experiences during many solitary wanderings while collecting information for this book would be worth the telling, but I preserve the memories for the time when I can no longer climb. One, however, returns insistently to mind......

I remember a sunny day in the wilderness of Ruthwaite Cove: I lay idly on the warm rocks alongside Hard Tarn, with desolation everywhere but in my heart, where was peace. The air was still; there was no sound, and nothing in view but the shattered confusion of rocks all around. I might have been the last man in a dead world. A tiny splash drew my gaze to the crystal-clear depths of the tarn ...... a newt was swimming there, just beneath the surface. I watched it for a long time. And I fell to wondering...... wondering about it, and its mission as it circled the smooth waters, and the purpose of its life – and mine. A trivial thing to remember, maybe, yet I do. I often think of that small creature, a speck of life in the immensity of desolation in which it had its being.'

The Eastern Fells, Some Personal Notes in conclusion

Hard Tarn
The Eastern Fells, Nethermost Pike, p. 4

Introduction

In his Personal Notes in conclusion to *The Eastern Fells*, Wainwright wrote: 'I suppose it might be said, to add impressiveness to the whole thing, that this book has been twenty years in the making.'

This book has been twelve years in the making, being conceived in 2011 after I edited The Wainwright Society's Challenge book. I was inspired to write my own book about Wainwright and sent an outline plan to John Nicoll, then owner of Francis Lincoln Limited, the publisher of Wainwright's books. John encouraged me to write the book, but the project was put on hold when I became Secretary of the Society in 2013.

Following my 'retirement' as Secretary in 2020, I returned to the idea of writing the book. But my ideas had changed after becoming a volunteer at Coleridge Cottage in Somerset, owned by the National Trust. The cottage was closed for the best part of 2020, during the Covid pandemic, and I took the opportunity of reading Richard Holmes' excellent biography of the poet. There was an intriguing reference to Wainwright in the book where Holmes compared the fellwalking exploits of Coleridge to those of Wainwright, stating that he believed that Wainwright could be Coleridge's 'greatest inheritor'.

I was so struck by this comparison that I began to look for other parallels between Wainwright and the Romantic poets, the most obvious being that both Coleridge and Wordsworth spent time in the Lake District walking on the fells and writing about landscape and Nature.

At the time, I had never read all of Wainwright's books, so I set to reading every book and published letter that he had ever written, a task that took the best part of two years. I compiled a list of themes that Wainwright and the Romantic poets had in common, particularly relating to their shared philosophy. I noted many references in Wainwright's books that mirrored their common beliefs.

In referring to Wainwright as a post-Romantic I have acknowledged that there is not complete commonality in their views as Wainwright lived in a different century and some elements of his philosophy do not have a direct comparison to the Romantic era. I hope that readers will forgive my indulgence in making those links between the two. …

* * * * * * *

Wainwright's enigmatic tale of a newt in Hard Tarn has always fascinated me. He recounts the story but does not offer an explanation of its significance apart from writing, 'I fell to wondering ...... wondering about it, and its mission as it circled the smooth waters, and the purpose of its life – and mine.' I have often thought that this was a significant moment in his life – perhaps as great as his epiphany on Orrest Head in 1930.

What was Wainwright's purpose and mission? He was far more than a writer of guidebooks. Having read every one of his million and a half published words, I am convinced that Wainwright's purpose and mission was to show his readers another way to live – a life in harmony with Nature and the natural world. For Wainright it was the way to peace of mind, true happiness and contentment, just as he found on that day in Ruthwaite Cove. It was a feeling of being at one with the landscape, discerning its moods and having an awareness of the need to respect Nature. Instinctively, he sensed the dangers of damaging the natural world – that somehow Nature would bite back. Perhaps he would not be surprised by the consequences of climate change?

His message was not strident, but quietly understated, perhaps hoping it would be absorbed gently into the psyche of his readers, that they would experience the same joy as he had in exploring the natural world, that they would find their own way. It was a message he shared with the Romantic poets of two centuries before.

* * * * * * *

Above all, this book is an appreciation of Wainwright's life and work, in particular his unique writing style in over fifty published books together with his incomparable penmanship in creating the many beautiful pen and ink drawings that illustrate his work.

Derek Cockell
March 2023

CHAPTER ONE

Wainwright: post-Romantic?

On 29th June 1800, Samuel Taylor Coleridge arrived in Grasmere with his wife Sara and their young son on his way to taking up residence at Greta Hall in Keswick. He was intending to continue a successful collaboration with William Wordsworth that had begun three years earlier when the two young poets lived in Somerset, publishing their first book of Romantic poetry, *Lyrical Ballads*.

Coleridge had been introduced to the Lake District the previous November when Wordsworth escorted him on a guided tour very much in the style of the early guidebook writers. In a letter he wrote to Wordsworth's sister, Dorothy, it is clear that the landscape had a deep emotional effect on him:

> 'You can feel what I cannot express for myself—how deeply I have been impressed by a world of scenery absolutely new to me. At Rydal & Grasmere I rec[eive]d I think the deepest delight, yet Hawes Water thro' many a varying view kept my eyes dim with tears, and this evening, approaching Derwentwater in diversity of harmonious features, in the majesty of its beauties & in the Beauty of its majesty—O my God! & the Black Crags close under the snowy mountains, whose snows were pinkish with the setting sun & the reflections from the sandy rich Clouds that floated over some and rested on others! It was to me a vision of a fair Country.'[1]

His reaction was very similar to Wainwright's emotional description of the mountains from the summit of Orrest Head on his first visit in 1930:

> 'It was a moment of magic, a revelation so unexpected that I stood transfixed, unable to believe my eyes. I saw mountain ranges, one after another, the nearer starkly etched, those beyond fading into the blue distance. Rich woodlands, emerald pastures

and the shimmering waters of the lake below added to a pageant of loveliness, a glorious panorama that held me enthralled.'[2]

But Coleridge was not content just to look at the landscape; he wanted to climb the mountains and explore the whole area. Two months after he had set up home in Keswick, he decided to visit the Wordsworths in Grasmere by walking the ridge from Clough Head to Helvellyn, descending by Raise Beck to Dunmail Raise in gathering darkness before taking to the road. Crossing the summit of Helvellyn he recorded in his Notebook his impressions of Striding Edge before making the descent:

> 'Am now at the Top of Helvellin ... travelling along the ridge I came to the other side of those precipices and down below me on my left—no—no! no words can convey any idea of this prodigious wildness/that precipice fine on this side was but its ridge, sharp as a (jagged) knife, level so long, and then ascending so boldly ... The Moon is above Fairfield almost at the full!— now descended over a perilous peat-moss then down a Hill of stones all dark, and darkling, I climbed stone after stone down a half dry Torrent and came out at the Raise Gap.'[3]

In his biography, *Coleridge, Early Visions*, Richard Holmes observed that: 'These prose notations were a new form of Romantic nature-writing, as powerful in their way as his poetry;' and in a footnote he added: 'The originality and power of Coleridge's fell-walking Notebooks and letters has only recently received some attention.... Among many other aspects, Coleridge is the first to introduce the impression of physical effort, travelling bodily through a landscape, and perilous immediacy (with the implied doubt that he will ever return). His greatest inheritor is, perhaps, Alfred Wainwright.'[4]

Coleridge's connection with Wainwright is their shared love of the Lake District and the emotive response to the landscape and Nature expressed in their writing. Like Wainwright, Coleridge was a prodigious walker. During the period 1800-03, he explored much of the district, climbing the mountains and recording details of his walks in his Notebooks and letters. Other travellers followed, some writing guidebooks to the more popular fells, but there was nobody like Wainwright, who explored the mountains so comprehensively and, like Coleridge, with such regard to the wonder, power and majesty of Nature.

William Wordsworth was a native of Cumberland, born in Cockermouth in 1770. After a year spent in Somerset with Coleridge (1797-8), he and his sister Dorothy moved back to the Lake District, first settling in Grasmere before moving to his final home at Rydal. Like Coleridge, his poetry celebrates the natural world and the landscape that formed the backdrop to his life.

Both Coleridge and Wordsworth were fascinated by tales and legends from the medieval period and some of their poems were either set in medieval times or retold stories from that era. In Wordsworth's poem, *Song at the Feast of Brougham Castle*, the War of the Roses is the setting. It tells how the son of John Clifford, who was killed at the Battle of Towton in 1461, was spirited away by his mother and sent into hiding with a trustworthy shepherd and brought up as his son. Lord Henry Clifford, known as the Shepherd Lord, had his estates and titles returned to him by Henry VII after the defeat of Richard III at the Battle of Bosworth in 1485. In the poem, Henry Clifford is depicted living in the Lake District as a shepherd and attended by the birds and animals:

> 'Our Clifford was a happy Youth,
> And thankful through a weary time,
> That brought him up to manhood's prime.
> —Again he wanders forth at will,
> And tends a Flock from hill to hill:[5]
> Yet lacks not friends for solemn glee,
> And a cheerful company,[6]
> To his side the Fallow-deer
> Came, and rested without fear;
> The Eagle, Lord of land and sea,
> Stooped down to pay him fealty;
> And both the undying fish that swim
> Through Bowscale-Tarn did wait on him,
> The pair were Servants of his eye
> In their immortality;'[7]

Wainwright was aware of these local legends and recounted the stories in his Pictorial Guides. In his chapter on Bowscale Fell, he wrote:

> 'Once upon a time it was fashionable to include a visit to Bowscale Tarn in the itineraries of Ladies and Gentlemen

making a Grand Tour of the Lakes. The tarn was famous for its two undying fish (an ancient tradition revived in a poem by Wordsworth), the setting was wild and romantic, and a good path led up to it . . . . . The walk is no longer popular. The story of the two immortal fish is almost forgotten, although, if it be true, they must still be there.'[8]

Bowscale Tarn from the north
The Northern Fells, Bowscale Fell, p. 2

The medieval period held a particular fascination for Wainwright. He regarded it as the high point of penmanship, when books were handwritten on vellum prior to the invention of the printing press in the 15th century.

He admired the craftsmen who built churches and other religious edifices that still stand today in parishes all over the country and he appreciated the skill of the countrymen who built humble farmhouses and sheepfolds in the vernacular style.

In Wainwright's body of work, he explores and documents the upland landscapes of Britain, whether it be his guidebooks to the Lake District, the Yorkshire Dales and the Pennines or his sketchbooks, describing the physical features of the hills and valleys and the impact that Nature and Man has had in shaping the landscape we see today. In all his work it is his emotional response to what he sees and feels that resonates most strongly with the poetry and philosophy of the Romantic writers.

He wrote also about the peace and tranquillity of mind and spirit that comes from climbing mountains, the beauty that is there for all to see in the valleys and hills, and the sense of awe and wonder that is felt in the high places. Landscape and Nature were two recurring themes of the Romantic poets; themes that are also prominent in Wainwright's work.

* * * * * * *

In a letter written in May 1942 to Eric Maudsley (a former work colleague at Blackburn) he seemed to identify with the Lakeland Romantic poets, implying he would be as famous one day:

> 'I agree with your remarks re Wainwright letters. They are good, unquestionably. Actually, you know, I came here to write and draw. Wordsworth and Wainwright, these two!'[9]

In another letter written in April 1943, Wainwright compares the work he is doing to that of the Lakeland poets, implying, somewhat tongue-in-cheek, that he will be remembered with them in the minds of his readers. He describes a visit to Shap Abbey where he enjoyed an hour contemplating the ruins set in a field of primroses, whilst listening to the sounds of Nature all around him, a world away from the army training ground that Eric was experiencing at that time:

> 'Future generations, when they think of Wordsworth and Southey and Coleridge and de Quincey, will think of Wainwright also. All my energies are now devoted to this aim. I am engaged on a work which will bring me fame, and enthusiasm for it is running white-hot; life is deliriously exciting. I haven't left myself time to tell you of my plan in detail, but believe me, this is Wainwright attaining a new best....
>
> Today my researches took me on a first visit to Shap, where, by the side of the infant Lowther, in a sleepy hollow of the fells, I spent an enjoyable hour amongst the primroses gazing at the ruins of the old Abbey. I wore flannels, not khaki. I listened to the myriad voices of nature, perfectly attuned, not to the raucous call of the sergeant-major.
>
> So leave me here with my dreams and my plans, in the Lakeland I love so passionately.'[10]

A Newt in Hard Tarn

Shap Abbey from the north
A Coast to Coast Walk, p. 56

Wainwright's writing is rooted in the shared philosophy of the Romantic poets, particularly Coleridge and Wordsworth. In his books and private correspondence his focus is on landscape and the natural world. At heart he was a post-Romantic, one whose writing embodied the spirit of the Romantic poets of the previous century.

NOTES

[1] *Collected Letters of Samuel Taylor Coleridge, Vol I*, edited by Earl Leslie Griggs, pp. 544-5

[2] *Ex-Fellwanderer*, unpaginated

[3] *The Notebooks of Samuel Taylor Coleridge, Vol 1*, edited by Kathleen Coburn, 798, f39-f41

[4] Richard Holmes, *Coleridge, Early Visions*, p. 281

[5] William Wordsworth, *Poems by William Wordsworth, Vol II*, 1815, p. 63 Lines 109-113

[6] William Wordsworth, *Poems by William Wordsworth, Vol II*, 1815, p. 63 Lines 118-119

[7] William Wordsworth, *Poems by William Wordsworth, Vol II*, 1815, pp. 63-4 Lines 122-129 Text of *Song at the Feast of Brougham Castle*, see website: https://en.wikisource.org/wiki/Page:Poems_by_William_Wordsworth_(1815)_Volume_2.djvu/66

[8] *The Northern Fells*, Bowscale Fell p. 7

[9] *The Wainwright Letters*, edited by Hunter Davies, p. 51

[10] *The Wainwright Letters*, edited by Hunter Davies, p. 70

CHAPTER TWO

Romantic Landscapes

During the second half of the eighteenth century, travel became easier as the road network was improved by the activities of the Turnpike Trusts. The more remote areas of the country such as the Lake District began to be visited by writers and accounts of their explorations appeared in print for the first time.

The early travellers may have been captivated by the scenery, seeking out viewpoints that illustrated picturesque views, but others recoiled from the sight of the craggy heights and tumultuous waterfalls. These first views of Nature in the raw induced emotions of awe, wonder and even terror, described philosophically as 'sublime' in the eighteenth century.

The term 'picturesque' was first described by William Gilpin as: 'that peculiar kind of beauty, which is agreeable in a picture'[1] – in other words, a landscape scene that was fit for an artist's frame. Sir Uvedale Price thought this description was too imprecise and argued that the qualities of the picturesque should include: 'roughness, . . . sudden variation [and] irregularity'[2]. Examples of the picturesque in the landscape included ancient buildings or structures, bridges, ruins, and objects from Nature such as rocks, crags, ancient or mature trees, waterfalls and fast-flowing streams or rivers.

In 1778, Thomas West published *A Guide to the Lakes*, the first of its kind, and dedicated it to: 'The lovers of landscape studies, and to all who have visited, or intend to visit, the Lakes in Cumberland, Westmorland, and Lancashire.'[3]

In his opening paragraphs, he made it clear that his Tour rivalled the *Grand Tour* of Europe that was popular at the time and that visitors would be able to follow in the footsteps of others who had already written accounts of this lovely part of northern England:

> '. . . there to contemplate, in Alpine scenery, finished in nature's highest tints, what refined art labours to imitate; the pastoral and rural landscape, varied in all the stiles, the soft, the rude, the

romantic and sublime. Combinations not found elsewhere assembled within so small a tract of country.' 4

The Guide was set out as visits to recommended viewpoints (called 'stations' in the book) where there followed a description of the view as in this example:

Borrowdale, from Castle Crag
A Fourth Lakeland Sketchbook, No. 300

'STATION IV. From the top of CASTLE-ROCK or crag, in BORROWDALE, there is a most astonishing view of the lake and vale of KESWICK, spread out to the north in the most picturesque manner. From the pass of BORROWDALE, every bend of the river, till it joins the lake, is distinctly seen; the lake itself, spotted with islands; the most extraordinary line of shore, varied with all the surprising accompanyments of rocks and woods; the village of GRANGE at the foot of the rock, and the white houses of KESWICK, with CROSTHWAITE church at the lower end of the lake; behind these much cultivation, with a beautiful mixture of villages, houses, cots, and farms, round the skirts of SKIDDAW, which rises in the grandest manner, from a verdant base, and closes this scene in the noblest stile of nature's true sublime.'[5]

'To the south, the view is in BORROWDALE. The river is seen winding from the lake upward, through the rugged pass, to where it divides and embraces a triangular vale, completely cut into inclosures of meadow, enameled with softest verdure, and fields waving with fruitful crops, the ample return to the laudable toil of the peaceful inhabitants. This truly secreted spot is completely surrounded by the most horrid, romantic mountains in this region of wonders; and whoever omits this COUP D' OEILE, [glance] hath seen nothing equal to it amongst the marvelous scenes.

The views here taken in the glass, in sunshine, are amazingly fine.'[6]

The Jaws of Borrowdale (centre left) and Castle Crag (centre right)
A Lakeland Sketchbook, No. 21

Words often change their meaning over time and using 'horrid' to describe the mountains means terrible or frightful in this context and expresses the emotional effect upon the viewer, similar to describing the landscape as 'sublime'. To reassure the reader, West goes on to explain that no other view is its equal in the District.

The 'glass' referred to in the final paragraph is a landscape mirror, usually known as a Claude glass, named after the landscape artist, Claude (Lorrain). It was a small convex mirror held close to the shoulder in order that the viewer might see the scene behind within the frame of the glass, rather like a landscape painting i.e. in true picturesque style!

The publication of West's *A Guide to the Lakes* was the beginning of popular tourism in the Lake District and gave rise to the term known as the *Picturesque Tour*. On his first visit to the Lake District in 1799, Coleridge described his walk with Wordsworth as his: 'pikteresk Toor'.[7]

* * * * * * *

In his appreciation of upland landscapes, Wainwright rarely used 'sublime' and 'picturesque', preferring the word 'romantic' in his descriptions. However, it is clear that his romantic landscapes included all the characteristics of the sublime and the picturesque whilst acknowledging the appeal to the senses, emotions and imagination which enabled him to link the present with those who had shaped the landscape in ages past.

In his book, *A Pennine Journey,* written in 1939 after a walking holiday in the Pennines, he described his intense emotion upon contemplating his first sight of Hadrian's Wall, which was his objective. What made the Wall so special was its association with historical events:

> 'Hadrian's Wall by this time had begun to acquire quite a new significance. I was eager to see it, not now only because it meant achievement of my aims, but because latterly my thoughts had invested it with romance; as I had come nearer to it so had my appreciation of the magnitude of the task undertaken by the Roman legions of long ago grown gradually keener. Whether I should find an imposing fortification, or a scrap of crumbling ruin, did not matter. I should see something that was as old as the Gospels, something that had withstood the ravages of time and tempest since the land was heathen. I should touch a stone that had not been moved since a long-forgotten Roman soldier placed it there, and I should think as I regarded it that there it had been in the days of Boadicea, there it had been in the days of William the Conqueror, there it had been when Royalists and Roundheads divided the land.

Romantic Landscapes

I knew I should be thrilled at the sight of the Wall, be it ever so disappointing in itself; its appeal was no longer to the eyes but to the imagination. But how foolish of me to be impatient, to wish the four hours fled! For nineteen centuries it had been awaiting me.'[8]

And on reaching the Wall the most romantic place was Cuddy's Crag, not just because of its history, but primarily for its dramatic situation, sinuously weaving its way along the edge of a steep escarpment. It was a place to savour, a place to recall on winter nights in his imagination when he returned home:

The Wall on Cuddy's Crag, looking east to Housesteads Crags
Pennine Way Companion, p. 34

'The north face of the Wall was soon on the edge of a precipitous cliff to which a few pines clung; as I went along, I could look down vertical clefts between rocky buttresses to rough scree far below. A false step here would be disastrous, but it is a glorious experience to traverse the very brink on so wonderful a path. This is Cuddy's Crag, the most romantic spot on the whole length of the Wall. It is a place to bring a fire to the dullest eyes, to inflame the most prosaic mind. For the person who is already under the spell, here is the perfect Elysium. Cuddy's Crag is a place to dream of by your fireside on a wild winter's night.'[9]

It was the physical characteristics of the landscape, its wild and rocky appearance with dark, menacing crags that could evoke feelings of awe and fear at the power and grandeur of Nature, as in this sketch by Wainwright of Dow Crag on a winter's day. Note how the two walkers help to give scale to the drawing and emphasise their insignificance in this inhospitable, sublime landscape:

Dow Crag and Goats Water
A Third Lakeland Sketchbook, No. 165

'The atmosphere of wild and romantic Lakeland, as portrayed by early artists, is nowhere better exemplified, especially on a stormy day, than at the outlet of Goats Water, where a chaotic tumble of boulders and the dark buttresses of Dow Crag frame a scene of stark desolation. This can be a fearful place.'[10]

Romantic Landscapes

Wainwright drew sketches of waterfalls in many of his books. One of the more spectacular is Aira Force in the Lake District. In a setting of mature woodland, the water plunges dramatically down a near-vertical rocky gorge draped with mosses and ferns, to a deep pool. In this example, the romantic atmosphere has been enhanced by the hand of man, the valley being landscaped in the 1780s and planted with thousands of native and ornamental trees. The two bridges mentioned were later additions:

Aira Force, Ullswater
A Lakeland Sketchbook, No. 16

'Aira Force is seldom without visitors; its proximity to the road and easy access, added to the beauty of wooded surroundings, make it a place of popular resort. Picturesque stone bridges above and below the waterfall enhance a romantic setting.'[11]

Old or ancient buildings were another characteristic of the picturesque aesthetic, and were often the subject of landscape artists. Wainwright had a fascination with the industrial ruins from another age and included drawings of them in his books. Abandoned mines, quarry huts, riverside mills and limestone kilns all featured in his work. He had a nostalgic love for the workplaces of lost rural ways of life and he delighted in preserving the memories in his sketches.

There were hamlets like Stonethwaite in the Borrowdale valley where the cottages added to the romantic charm of the scenery:

Stonethwaite
A Fourth Lakeland Sketchbook, No. 277

'Beyond [Borrowdale church] a no-through lane leads into the short side valley of Stonethwaite to a scene that has resisted change in a changing world and still retains the romantic charm of three centuries ago; the mellowed stones of its buildings and walls blend in perfect harmony with a delightful landscape of pastures and woodlands and colourful fells while a crystal beck provides the musical symphony.'[12]

Occasionally, it was not just the building that stirred his emotions, it was its location in the landscape. Black Sail Hut is situated in a vast amphitheatre at the head of Ennerdale, the only habitation for four lonely miles and remote from settlements in adjoining valleys.

Originally, it was a shepherd's bothy but was acquired by the YHA and converted into a Youth Hostel. Wainwright included it as a possible stopping place on his Coast to Coast Walk.

Black Sail Hut at the head of Ennerdale[13]
A Fourth Lakeland Sketchbook, No. 272

Wainwright revisited Black Sail Hut in a television series celebrating the Coast to Coast Walk, filmed in 1988. As they approached, he said to Eric Robson: 'You've arrived at the Black Sail Hut in the middle of a grand surround of mountains including Great Gable, Kirk Fell, Pillar, Haystacks, the High Stile ridge behind you. . . . It's the loneliest, most romantic spot in the Lake District. If you're a walker it's ideal. Splendid week's walking from here . . . different mountain every day. No traffic. No crowds. No litter. Wonderful place.'[14]

Wainwright loved the Black Sail Hut primarily for its remote, romantic location and also for it being fortunate to be encircled by a group of mountains whose names captured the imagination of walkers and lovers of Lakeland.

Ashness Bridge was a packhorse bridge on the road to the hidden valley of Watendlath. It was built in the eighteenth century, but very soon after the first tourists arrived it became a favoured location for its picturesque views of Derwentwater backed by the Skiddaw range.

In this sketch, the view has all the qualities of 'roughness, sudden variation and irregularity' that is the embodiment of the picturesque: large angular rocks and boulders, an old rough-hewn stone bridge, fast-flowing water in Ashness Gill, silhouettes of mature trees in winter and a serrated skyline of snow-covered mountains.

Wainwright described this view as 'soft beauty'[15] in a letter he sent to his friend, Lawrence Wolstenholme in 1949 together with a copy of the sketch of Ashness Bridge:

Ashness Bridge
A Fifth Lakeland Sketchbook, No. 386

'One of the most photographed scenes in Lakeland is the perfect composition provided by the picturesque Ashness Bridge on the romantic road to Watendlath. Had the scene been specially designed for the camera it could not have been better; it is a gem. The Skiddaw group form an impressive background to a beautiful view.'[16]

Romantic Landscapes

Wainwright considered the road to Watendlath the most romantic road in Lakeland. It was narrow and branched off the valley road in Borrowdale to head uphill before descending into a hidden valley leading to the Lakeland farm of Watendlath, the fictional home of Judith Paris in the *Herries Chronicles*, written by Hugh Walpole in the 1930s:

The road to Watendlath
A Lakeland Sketchbook, No. 6

'The most enchanting and romantic of all Lakeland's roads is the narrow byway leaving Borrowdale at Ashness Gate and ending at Watendlath, four miles away in a fold of the hills.'[17]

The gateway shown in the sketch was the site of Low Strutta Gate, named by Wainwright in *The Central Fells* as: 'Vivian Fisher's gate'.[18] In his final book, *Wainwright in the Valleys of Lakeland*, he revealed the story behind the alternative name, which added to the romantic charm of the road to Watendlath:

'Older readers may remember the benign figure of Vivian Fisher who presided at the first gate across the road above the junction for many years after the war. Rosy cheeked, happy and smiling, he had a friendly greeting for all who came along as he opened the gate for them to pass through in anticipation of a reward, and with true business sense closed it immediately after them although others were approaching. He had a ready conversation and would recite poems or sing songs if requested, and sometimes if not. He was a man attuned to nature, sharing his sandwiches with the many chaffinches who hovered around him and never failing to extol the beauties of Lakeland. . . . He was a rare character and the Ashness Gate always seem[ed] forlorn after his death.'[19]

There was an indefinable quality about romantic landscapes, an atmosphere that Wainwright described as romantic charm. And nowhere was that enchantment felt more than in the Lake District, his own personal heaven on earth. In a somewhat contrite Introduction to *A North Wales Sketchbook*, he felt he had to explain his devotion to Lakeland in preference to the mountains of Snowdonia:

'Since early in life I have been a devout admirer of the English Lake District, enslaved by the loveliness of this romantic fairyland. The mountains have been the shrines where I have worshipped, the valleys the haunts where I have wandered in utter contentment; the dancing becks have been my symphonies, the lakes my glittering jewels. In Lakeland beauty is all around, everything is in harmony. There is magic in the air and I have been under its spell. Lakeland is my home, my heaven.'[20]

Perhaps Wainwright came closest to defining what he meant by romantic charm in his description of Borrowdale, a valley that, for him, epitomised the 'romantic loveliness' of the Lake District:

'Borrowdale is the very heart of the Lake District and here the romantic loveliness of the region is fully displayed. It is the most beautiful of the valleys, fair to look upon throughout its length from the colourful mountains at its head to the charming lake of Derwentwater in its lower reaches. Everywhere is a mystic delight that dims the eyes with tears of joy and uplifts the spirit in exultation. Its great appeal is that it is unorthodox, following no pattern but forming a haphazard landscape of craggy outcrops, verdant woodlands and emerald pastures watered by a crystal river, of hanging gardens of rowan and birch above a floor of mature oaks, with a scattering of white cottages and farmhouses that in no way intrudes but fits perfectly into a picture of rural tranquillity. Nature has been bountiful in Borrowdale: this is its showplace, a heaven on earth.'[21]

The natural elements combine in a haphazard arrangement that typifies the romantic charm of the Lake District. Those elements are: craggy outcrops, verdant woodlands comprising native trees such as rowan, birch and oaks and emerald pastures all threaded together by the crystal water of the River Derwent that flows down the valley to the sparkling lake of Derwentwater.

But this valley is not wild and desolate. Here Man has worked with Nature in harmony to create a landscape where settlements have grown organically over the centuries; where there is a sense of a long occupation and where Nature has softened the buildings with moss and lichen and mature trees, providing habitats for a diverse population of plants and animals. Man-made structures – buildings, stone walls, barns and bridges – have been constructed by craftsmen using local materials that blend into, and are in harmony with, the natural landscape of craggy mountains.

Wander in Borrowdale and the spirit is uplifted, emotions are stirred and one is left with an overwhelming sense of peace, contentment and well-being. Wainwright described these feelings as 'a mystic delight that dims the eyes with tears of joy and uplifts the spirit in exultation'. He believed that the only way to experience those feelings and emotions was to immerse oneself in the landscape, to walk on the hills, alone and in silence. Only then would the solitary walker feel the spirit of the high places and be blessed.

NOTES

[1] William Gilpin, *An Essay Upon Prints*, 1768, p. xii
See full text: https://archive.org/details/anessayonprints00gilpgoog/mode/2up

[2] Sir Uvedale Price, *On the Picturesque*, 1794, p. 61
See full text: https://archive.org/details/essayonpicturesq01pric/page/60/mode/2up

A Newt in Hard Tarn

[3] Thomas West, *A Guide to the Lakes*, 1778, Dedication
[4] Thomas West, *A Guide to the Lakes*, 1778, pp. 1-2
[5] Thomas West, *A Guide to the Lakes*, 1778, p. 97
[6] Thomas West, *A Guide to the Lakes*, 1778, pp. 98-9
[7] *The Notebooks of Samuel Taylor Coleridge, Vol 1*, edited by Kathleen Coburn, 508
[8] *A Pennine Journey*, p. 89
[9] *A Pennine Journey*, p. 110
[10] *A Third Lakeland Sketchbook*, No. 165
[11] *A Lakeland Sketchbook*, No. 16
[12] *Wainwright in the Valleys of Lakeland*, p. 195
[13] Black Sail Hut is located just to the left of the trees where they end at the head of the valley
[14] *Wainwright's Coast to Coast Walk*, BBC Worldwide Ltd., 2003, Programme 1, St Bees Head to Haweswater (first screened in 1989)
[15] *The Wainwright Letters*, edited by Hunter Davies, p. 77
[16] *Fellwalking with a Camera*, unpaginated
[17] *A Lakeland Sketchbook*, No. 6
[18] *The Central Fells*, High Seat p. 3
[19] *Wainwright in the Valleys of Lakeland*, p. 202
[20] *A North Wales Sketchbook*, Introduction
[21] *Wainwright's Coast to Coast Walk*, p. 47

CHAPTER THREE

Solitary Walker

It was only on rare occasions that Wainwright would accept the companionship of others on his walks. By nature, he was happy in his own company, preferring to walk alone. Someone who was permitted to join Wainwright on a walk was Weaver Owen, the bank manager of Lloyds Bank in Kendal. He recounted the circumstances to Hunter Davies (author of *Wainwright The Biography*) in 1994:

> "'Some time in 1949 we found ourselves standing at the same bus stop one Sunday morning on the Windermere Road, . . . I'd always been a keen walker and before the war spent all my holidays youth hostelling. I kept on meeting AW, on the same bus, and now and again we found we were planning to go on the same walk. The first walk we did together was up Nab Scar which he found heavy going.'"[1]

Weaver Owen corresponded with Wainwright in 1986, congratulating him on the success of the BBC television series. He recalled their first meeting, and included a quotation from the essayist, William Hazlitt:

> 'I first met you in 1949 in your official capacity as a borough treasurer and also as a walker waiting for the same bus on a Sunday morning at the Windermere road stop. How we ever came to have a walk together is wrapped in mystery as we both shared Hazlitt's view on walking:- "One of the pleasantest things in the world is going a journey; but I like to be by myself. I can enjoy society in a room; but out of doors, nature is company enough for me. I am then never less alone than when alone. I cannot see the wit of walking and talking at the same time."'[2]

William Hazlitt was a contemporary of Coleridge and Wordsworth and knew them both well. He wrote his essay, *On Going a Journey*, in 1822, in which he extolled the virtues of solitary walking. Its influence was demonstrated when over fifty years later it was praised in an article by Robert Louis Stevenson, writing that Hazlitt's essay was: 'so good that there should be a tax levied on all who have not read it'.[3]

Solitary walking and walking tours were often used by the Romantic poets as vehicles for putting forward philosophical arguments about God, Nature, Man and Society.

The Excursion, by William Wordsworth, is a poem based on the discussions that take place on a walking tour in the Lake District by the three main characters: the Author, the Wanderer and the Solitary.

Bleatarn House
A Fourth Lakeland Sketchbook, No. 250

In the poem, the Author and the Wanderer, visit the Solitary, a Scottish Presbyterian Minister, who now lives as a shepherd in the cottage, known as Bleatarn House, where he entertains his guests with lunch of cheese, oat-cakes and fruit. After spending the night in the cottage, they leave together the following morning.

In one passage, they discuss the negative effects of the Industrial Revolution on landscape, Nature and family life. Landscape conservation and the protection of Nature were matters close to Wainwright's heart:

> *Industrialisation of the countryside*
> 'Meanwhile, at social Industry's command,
> How quick, how vast an increase! From the germ
> Of some poor Hamlet, rapidly produced
> Here a huge Town, continuous and compact,
> Hiding the face of earth for leagues—and there,
> Where not a Habitation stood before,
> The Abodes of men irregularly massed
> Like trees in forests,—spread through spacious tracts,
> O'er which the smoke of unremitting fires
> Hangs permanent, and plentiful as wreaths
> Of vapour glittering in the morning sun.
> And, wheresoe'er the Traveller turns his steps,
> He sees the barren wilderness erased,'
>
> *The damaging effects of industrialisation on Nature*
> 'With You I grieve, when on the darker side
> Of this great change I look; and there behold ...
> Such outrage done to Nature as compels
> The indignant Power to justify herself;
> Yea, to avenge her violated rights,
> For England's bane.—When soothing darkness spreads
> O'er hill and vale,'
>
> *The effects of industrialisation on family life*
> 'Lo! in such neighbourhood, from morn to eve,
> The Habitations empty! or perchance
> The Mother left alone,—no helping hand
> To rock the cradle of her peevish babe;
> No daughters round her, busy at the wheel,
> Or in dispatch of each day's little growth
> Of household occupation; no nice arts
> Of needle-work; no bustle at the fire,
> Where once the dinner was prepared with pride;
> Nothing to speed the day, or cheer the mind;'[4]

* * * * * * *

Wainwright's first book, *A Pennine Journey*, shares similarities with Wordsworth's poem, being a philosophic journey set within the framework of a walking tour in the Pennines undertaken in 1938.

It is important to understand the background to the walk as it explains one of the main reasons why Wainwright undertook this 210-mile, 11-day marathon. It was a turbulent time in his personal life, with problems in his marriage and he felt he had nobody he could confide in to help ease the burden. His answer was to escape from an unhappy home life by taking his holidays alone where he would spend his time walking to his physical limits. It was a cathartic experience.

He explained his reasoning in a previously unknown autobiographical narrative written in the third person that was uncovered in 1994 by Hunter Davies when he was undertaking research for his biography of Wainwright:

> 'He spent his holidays alone always, and came to look forward to these stolen opportunities of temporary escape with real expectancy and eagerness. They meant a change of environment and he welcomed them joyfully. Inactive holidays he did not consider: he lived them to the full, and planned beforehand every minute of his liberation. He was mentally tired; his release lay in exercise for the body. They were no ordinary holidays he indulged in. The essential was change, and he sought all chances of making the change complete. A body that was habitually inactive was on these occasions flogged into weariness by excessive effort; he found a curious pleasure in physical exhaustion, accompanied as it always was by a mind at last at rest. He liked to be constantly on the move, spending each night in different surroundings; it irked to have to return to a familiar abode. So with a body as restless as his thoughts had been previously, he wandered from one scene to another....'[5]

The narrative of *A Pennine Journey* describes in detail his walk and the people he met along the way and is punctuated with philosophical asides on many subjects including his views about walking. This example explains why it is important to have an objective on a walk:

'Well now, having quite decided that this year I would see as much as I could of the Pennine country, I looked about for an objective in the North, a point on which my travels should focus, a place to attain and turn back from. I wanted to go north, and keep on going north as long as I could, but I had to remember that every step I took in that direction must of necessity be reversed later. I did not want, however, to start out without a plan, because without a programme I find myself cursed by indecision. I didn't want simply to go north until I was tired of going north, and turn in my tracks and come back. This might have happened in a field, in the middle of a moor, in a village street, anywhere. No, I must fix a point somewhere in the north, and attain it whatever happened, otherwise there would be . . . no sense of satisfaction to my homeward march. . . .

Much that I have just written is at direct variance with the accepted tradition of walkers which upholds that a person who loves walking will walk anywhere, just as his fancy pleases; he will refuse to be a slave to any programme, and will follow any byway that tempts his mood. I never do that; I couldn't. I'd rather stay at home than ramble aimlessly. I must have an objective, otherwise I derive no pleasure from walking. It doesn't matter in the least what the objective is: it may be the pillar box at the end of the road, a cricket match a few miles away, a signpost on a moorland track. It must be something to aim at. The most natural objective, to me, is a cairn of stones on the summit of a hill. Whatever it may be, it is decided upon before I move a step, and having decided upon it, nothing on earth can persuade me from it. . . . For success comes only from first deciding on your target, and refusing to be tempted from it; from attaining it in spite of all the hardships and tribulations on the way.'[6]

It was an argument that he returned to in the Introduction of his guide to another of his long-distance walks, *A Coast to Coast Walk*, written thirty-three years later:

'One should always have a definite objective, in a walk as in life – it is so much more satisfying to reach a target by personal effort than to wander aimlessly. An objective is an ambition, and life without ambition is . . . . . well, aimless wandering.'[7]

It could be argued that many of Wainwright's books, and in particular his guides and the large format series he wrote in the 1980s, are, at heart, philosophic rambles over the high places of Britain.

* * * * * * *

When Wainwright asked: 'Why does a man climb mountains?'[8] in his Soliloquy on Scafell Pike, it was not a rhetorical question. After decades of hillwalking, he had come to believe that there was a simple truth about man and his relationship with upland landscapes. In climbing a hill or a mountain, one's being becomes part of the landscape and attuned to the natural world and its rhythms.

Human perception of the physical world is made manifest through the senses: the sting of incessant rain on an upturned face, weathered rock beneath the feet, swirling mist enveloping craggy tops. It is the physical experience of being in the hills that builds up our cognitive understanding of the landscape and the prevailing conditions, which allows the mind to perceive, understand and make decisions such as turning back if the weather worsens or finding a safer descent route.

Whereas these physical sensations could be experienced and enjoyed on a walk with others (preferably, only one other person, who was quiet[9]), Wainwright came to understand that the landscape invoked an emotional response best appreciated by the solitary walker. He put it like this:

> 'It is the man or woman who walks alone who enjoys the greatest rewards, who sees and feels and senses the mood of the hills and knows them most intimately, . . . To the man in a conducted party the mountains are prose, to the man travelling alone they are poetry.'[10]

There are passages in the Pictorial Guides that express a sense of awe and wonder that he found in the majestic mountain scenery of places such as Great End. Wainwright makes it very clear to the reader that these moving experiences live on in the memory and can be recalled vividly long after returning home:

> 'When mist wreathes the summit and clings like smoke in the gullies, when ravens soar above the lonely crags, when snow lies deep and curtains of ice bejewel the gaunt cliffs, then Great End

is indeed an impressive sight. Sunshine never mellows this grim scene but only adds harshness.

This is the true Lakeland of the fellwalker, the sort of terrain that calls him back time after time, the sort of memory that haunts his long winter exile.

It is not the pretty places – the flowery lanes of Grasmere or Derwentwater's wooded bays – that keep him restless in his bed; it is the magnificent ones.

Places like Great End . . . . .'[11]

Great End, from Styhead Tarn
A Third Lakeland Sketchbook, No. 174

It was experiences like these on his solitary explorations that inspired Wainwright to convey to others his love of Lakeland and its varied landscapes in his writing and drawing. But he also realised that walking and climbing on the hills was good for his mental well-being, although he did not describe it in this way. In *Fellwanderer*, he wrote:

'Up here, one stands back from a too-familiar environment like a painter before his canvas and views events in true perspective. Friday's worries are seen to be nothing, after all. The only things that matter are immediate: the next foothold, the drifting mist, the darkening sky. Life is challenging, and, stripped of its pretences, life is good. With climbing comes an uplift, not only of

A Newt in Hard Tarn

the body but of the spirit and the mind. There is no competition here with one's fellows, no silly jealousies of the man in the next salary grade; one's aspirations are simple and decent. There is no worshipping of false idols on the mountains, but, instead, deep awareness of a Creator.'[12]

Wainwright believed that it was the solitary walker who appreciated the spiritual quality of being in the mountains. He was instinctively drawn to the connection between the natural world of weatherworn rock, swirling mist and reality: '. . . this was real. This was truth.'[13] Whatever troubled him in his everyday life, Wainwright found solace in the hills.

* * * * * * *

Much as he preferred to be climbing and walking in the rocky terrain of south-west Lakeland (five of his six favourite mountains lay in this sector) he was drawn to the quieter parts such as the northern fells because they were more remote and the very nature of the landscape attracted fewer visitors. He dedicated *The Northern Fells* to: 'those who travel alone THE SOLITARY WANDERERS ON THE FELLS who find contentment in the companionship of the mountains and of the creatures of the mountains'.[14]

Skiddaw Forest
A Fourth Lakeland Sketchbook, No. 283

'Skiddaw Forest is a forest without a tree, the word having its older meaning: a hunting ground. Apart from the lonely Skiddaw House (shepherds' cottages) here is a desolation profound, but it is a natural desolation, one with a beauty of its own and a strong appeal to the solitary walker.'[15]

In *The Northern Fells* he revealed that, Blencathra and Skiddaw apart, he had seen only one other walker on the other fells during his explorations and he wondered if anyone would buy the book, but went on to explain that this was how he liked it:

'These two apart, the only other fell on which I saw another person in the whole of my walks, and then at a distance, was Carrock Fell, and this happened on three different occasions. As for the rest – nobody, not a soul, not once. I felt I was preparing a book that would have no readers at all, a script that would have no players and no public. Nevertheless, these were glorious days for me – days of absolute freedom, days of feeling like the only man on earth. No crowds to dodge, no noisy chatter, no litter. Just me, and the sheep, and singing larks overhead. All of us well content.'[16]

Another group of hills that Wainwright loved, for their peace and tranquillity, was the Howgill Fells. Prior to the opening of the M6 motorway in 1970, the Howgills were known mainly to rail travellers en route to Scotland, with dramatic views of the western aspect of the range. As with the Lakeland fells, there was open access, but with few obstructions such as stone walls or fences. However, that fact could bring its own problems of route-finding in poor weather conditions, with few landmarks to aid the walker. Given that few people walked on these fells, in this instance, Wainwright advised walking with a companion:

'The heights in the south are well enough known to Sedbergh folk and to the boys of Sedbergh School particularly, but otherwise are visited only by a few discerning walkers who appreciate their quietness and seclusion. . . . One can walk all day here knowing full well that not another soul will be seen, and that one's footsteps may never again be trodden for years. It is the utter loneliness of the surroundings that constitutes the one (and only) hazard for the solitary walker, not the menace of crags or rough ground. In fact conditions underfoot are everywhere delightfully easy and objective dangers are absent. But a companion is advised – just in case. . . . In mist the wilder places should really be left alone. The central mass of high ground can be confusing, even in clear weather, because of the similarity of the various summits and an absence of distinguishing features, while the descending ridges conform to a common pattern, so that without constant reference to the map it is easy to wander hopelessly off course; . . .'[17]

The southern Howgill Fells
A Lune Sketchbook, No. 33

Despite these warnings, Wainwright wanted to encourage more people to visit and explore the Howgill Fells as he thought their very remoteness and solitude were an antidote to modern living, particularly with more people visiting the Lake District and the Dales:

'As yet the Howgills are relatively unknown. They are not, and never will be, a popular magnet, and in this lack of general appeal lies their great attraction for those who want to escape from the noise and the crowds. Here is a pervading tranquillity. . . . their greatest appeal must ever be to those who love to walk freely 'over the tops' and commune with nature in solitude. There is no better place for doing this than the Howgill Fells, bless them.'[18]

On the more popular fells in Lakeland he had, often, to share the summit with large groups of people such as his experience on Coniston Old Man where an excited group of tourists was shown pointing out Blackpool Tower!

The Summit
The Southern Fells, Coniston Old Man, p. 13

In a letter to Molly Lefebure written in 1970, he complained about the behaviour of walkers that he and Betty[19] had to endure on the summit of Great Gable:

> 'Mind you, the summit of Great Gable was no place to be that day. All the decent walkers are doing the limestone country this year, of course, unfortunately leaving in possession of Lakeland an untidy and noisy rabble of school parties and dropouts. You would have thought there was a Pop Festival going on, on top of Gable. There were hundreds of near-humans draped all over the summit, a noisy, uncouth, illiterate mob with transistors going full blast, and after a brief visit to Westmorland Cairn we fled the place.'[20]

In *Fellwanderer*, Wainwright explained that he needed to work undisturbed and, as the Pictorial Guides became more widely known, his fans began to anticipate where he would be working and set out to find him. But as he explained:

> 'I had work to do—maps to check, details of ascents to note, photographs to take, views to record—and could not afford distractions.'[21]

So he began to adopt strategies to avoid meeting people:

> 'On the more popular fells I had to observe many subterfuges to keep out of other people's way. If a summit was already occupied upon arrival I had to hang about in the vicinity until it was vacated. If others were coming along my path I wandered off it a while, behind a wall or a boulder, to avoid conversation.'[22]

He devised unconventional ploys in order to escape unwanted attention, describing one such experience in a letter to Molly Lefebure in 1965:

> 'Heaven preserve us from breezy individuals! The thing to do is to reverse the embarrassment. Memorise a short passage from a book on geology – just a sentence or two chosen at random – and carry a small hammer. Then when you find yourself being overtaken by someone who is obviously going to give you a hearty greeting, even if he doesn't actually slap you on the shoulder, as he strides past, just stop in your tracks and start tapping the nearest stone. The odds are he will pass without comment, but if he should ask what you are doing, look him up and down pityingly, quote your passage, and resume your concentration. He will creep quietly away! I know, I've tried it!'[23]

Occasionally, he spent nights on the fells in order to have an early start the following morning. With a dawn start he could be sure of seeing no other walkers until late morning.

One of his most memorable nights on the fells was spent on the slopes of Harrison Stickle in 1949. In the early evening he sat and watched a fox playing and rolling on a grassy shelf below him. The night was misty with a drizzling rain, but in the morning he was rewarded with a most glorious sunrise with mist filling the valley. He wrote excitedly to Lawrence Wolstenholme giving him all the details:

> 'The crazy season is in full swing – that of spending nights alone on the mountains. The weather has aided and abetted wonderfully this summer, and the exciting memories I have hoarded up for old age (which seems as far off as ever!) are pearls beyond price. Best of all, perhaps, was a glorious red sunrise seen from Harrison Stickle in a purple sky, while Langdale below was choked with cotton-wool clouds and seemed like a huge curving glacier, from the sheepfold below Rossett to Loughrigg, where it was joined by another glacier coming down from Grasmere. Out of this sea of white cloud rose all the familiar peaks of Lakeland, curiously detached, but warm and rosy and friendly in the early sunlight.'[24]

Harrison Stickle
The Central Fells, Harrison Stickle, p. 2

Experiences like these sharpened Wainwright's appreciation of the natural world and its enchanting beauty. In the hills, alone, he was at one with Nature and at peace. This was surely heaven on earth.

NOTES

[1] Hunter Davies, *Wainwright The Biography*, p. 124

[2] Letter from Weaver Owen to Alfred Wainwright, 13th June 1986 (unpublished)
See the full text of *On Going A Journey*: https://sites.ualberta.ca/~dmiall/Travel/hazlitt.htm
3rd January 1999

[3] Robert Louis Stevenson, *Walking Tours*, originally published in the Cornhill Magazine, 1876. Later included in the collection Virginibus Puerisque, and Other Papers (1881)
See article by Richard Nordquist and full text of *Walking Tours*: ThoughtCo, 11th October 2021, https://www.thoughtco.com/walking-tours-by-robert-louis-stevenson-1690301

[4] William Wordsworth, *The Excursion*, 1814, Book VIII, pp. 364-5 Lines 117-129, p. 366 Lines 151-158 & p. 371 Lines 265-274
Text of *The Excursion*, *see* website:
https://en.wikisource.org/wiki/Page:The_Excursion,_Wordsworth,_1814.djvu/385

[5] Hunter Davies, *Wainwright The Biography*, pp. 55-6
The manuscript is housed in the Kendal Archive Centre: Ref: WDAW/1/24/1 pp. 40-1

[6] *A Pennine Journey*, pp. 27-8

[7] *A Coast to Coast Walk*, Introduction p. iv

[8] *The Southern Fells*, Scafell Pike p. 24

[9] Wainwright wrote about walking with a companion in *A Pennine Journey*. He wrote of the advantages of choosing a quiet person: 'No; it is the quiet man you want. The best friend is the man who can walk along with you mile after mile and say not a word; in fact, silence is the great test of companionship.' *A Pennine Journey* p. 187

[10] *Fellwanderer*, unpaginated

[11] *The Southern Fells*, Great End p. 2

[12] *Fellwanderer*, unpaginated

[13] *Ex-Fellwanderer*, unpaginated
This quotation describes Wainwright's reactions to his first view of Lakeland from the summit of Orrest Head on 7th June 1930. 'I had seen landscapes of rural beauty pictured in the local art gallery, but here was no painted canvas; this was real. This was truth. God was in his heaven that day and I a humble worshipper.'

[14] *The Northern Fells*, Dedication

[15] *A Fourth Lakeland Sketchbook*, No. 283

[16] *The Northern Fells*, Some Personal Notes in conclusion

[17] *Walks on the Howgill Fells and adjoining fells*, The Howgill Fells, Introduction

[18] *Walks on the Howgill Fells and adjoining fells*, The Howgill Fells, Introduction

[19] Betty McNally was Wainwright's second wife. They were married on 10th March 1970

[20] *The Wainwright Letters*, edited by Hunter Davies, pp. 238-9

[21] *Fellwanderer*, unpaginated

[22] *Fellwanderer*, unpaginated

[23] *The Wainwright Letters*, edited by Hunter Davies, p. 144

[24] *The Wainwright Letters*, edited by Hunter Davies, p. 78

CHAPTER FOUR

Awakening to Beauty

In Ancient Greek culture, beauty was defined in objective terms based on mathematical notions of proportion, symmetry and harmony found in the natural world. The design of their public buildings, temples, statues and sculptures reflected these philosophical ideas. This objective view of beauty would continue to influence artists and architects for many centuries.

During the eighteenth century, ideas and established beliefs about what constituted beauty began to be challenged. Philosophers such as David Hume and Immanuel Kant began to argue that there could be a more subjective definition of beauty, one that related to the pleasure or happiness experienced by individuals when observing the natural world.

For some Romantic poets the changing world of industrialisation, the steady growth of towns and cities together with the drift of people away from the countryside inspired a belief that a return to Nature was essential, for it was argued that only an appreciation and love of natural beauty brought happiness and joy to the human spirit.

William Wordsworth expressed these ideas in a poem published in *Lyrical Ballads*, the first book of English Romantic poetry produced in collaboration with Samuel Taylor Coleridge in 1798. *Lines composed a few miles above Tintern Abbey*[1] is a poem that takes the speaker back to the landscape of the Wye valley that he had visited five years previously when he was a boy:

> 'Five years have past; five summers, with the length
> Of five long winters! and again I hear
> These waters, rolling from their mountain-springs
> With a soft inland murmur.—Once again
> Do I behold these steep and lofty cliffs,
> Which on a wild secluded scene impress
> Thoughts of more deep seclusion; and connect
> The landscape with the quiet of the sky.'[2]

He describes the joy of revisiting a landscape he loved and that brings to mind that he has felt that same happiness in the intervening years by recalling the scenes of his youthful wandering:

> 'Though absent long,
> These forms of beauty, have not been to me
> As is a landscape to a blind man's eye:
> But oft, in lonely rooms, and mid the din
> Of towns and cities, I have owed to them,
> In hours of weariness, sensations sweet,
> Felt in the blood, and felt along the heart;
> And passing even into my purer mind
> With tranquil restoration:
>
> How oft, in spirit, have I turned to thee,
> O sylvan Wye! Thou wanderer through the woods,
> How often has my spirit turned to thee!'[3]

The speaker acknowledges that when a boy, his joy was communing with Nature in a beautiful landscape, but with maturity he has come to understand the importance of the beauty of Nature to his inner happiness:

> 'Therefore am I still
> A lover of the meadows and the woods
> And mountains; and of all that we behold
> From this green earth; of all the mighty world
> Of eye, and ear,—both what they half-create,
> And what perceive;
>
> Knowing that Nature never did betray
> The heart that loved her; 'tis her privilege,
> Through all the years of this our life, to lead
> From joy to joy: for she can so inform
> The mind that is within us, so impress
> With quietness and beauty, and so feed
> With lofty thoughts, that neither evil tongues,
> Rash judgments, nor the sneers of selfish men,
> Nor greetings where no kindness is, nor all
> The dreary intercourse of daily life,

Shall e'er prevail against us, or disturb
Our chearful faith, that all which we behold
Is full of blessings.'[4]

Tintern Abbey
A South Wales Sketchbook, No. 6

Six months after he had moved to Kendal, at the end of November 1941, Wainwright expressed similar sentiments in a letter he wrote to his friend, Eric Maudsley:

'The thing most worth seeking in life, Eric, is beauty. Make no mistake about that. I couldn't be persuaded to swop this existence for any other. I have reached the foot of the rainbow, and here, sure enough, is the pot of gold I have been seeking – beauty so exquisite that it makes the heart leap with exultation, loveliness so enchanting that it brings tears to the eyes. This is wealth, real wealth; it is free of tax, and it is mine forever.'[5]

It was a statement of Wainwright's belief that natural beauty brought true happiness and contentment. His reaction came from the heart; an emotional response to the beauty and his love of the Lake District landscape that would last a lifetime.

* * * * * * *

In October 1939, just after the outbreak of war, Wainwright wrote a secret 'autobiography'.[6] It began with a description of Blackburn, the town in which he had been born and had lived all his life. It was an industrial cotton town, dirty, smoky, and, for Wainwright, a place without hope of happiness or peace in his heart:

> 'A cold wind had swept over the town from the north throughout the day, bringing with it sudden gusts of rain; a bitter wind which drove pitilessly along the deserted streets, swirled and eddied in doorways and alleys, and finally fled shrieking across the desolate moors beyond.
>
> Dark ragged fingers of cloud, mobile fractions of the grey leaden mass obscuring the sky, had driven furiously over the tops of the houses since long before the dawn: an unceasing disorderly procession sweeping along in confusion, responsive to every whim of its master, the wind. The smoke from thirty thousand chimneys was caught up before it escaped from the grimy roofs and swirled away to merge with the scudding clouds overhead, or to lose itself amongst the soaking pavements and sidewalks, there to add to the gloom.
>
> At no time had there been a lightening of the heavens: the valley was encompassed, shut in, by the drab wet pall that laid siege to it; there was no escape. The town had been strangely quiet all day, as though it realised the oppression of the heavy sky that seemed to have fallen almost on top of it, and submitted meekly, acknowledging defeat. Not for a month or more, since the outbreak of war, had the scream of the factory sirens been heard in the valley, and today the noise of the traffic had seemed subdued also. The street lamps no longer shed their yellow gleam through the murky air, but today lights had burned in the offices and workshops, behind darkened windows, at noon.
>
> Few people ventured about the streets after the workers had scurried home at dusk. Those who of necessity had to be out-of-doors hastened along noiselessly, appearing from the gloom like

ghosts and vanishing again as silently. A sudden unheralded downpour would send them running into the cheerless shelter afforded by shop doorways, where they stood shivering until they could take advantage of a temporary respite to hurry on their way.

Now, at eight o'clock, three hours after the gloom of the day had merged into the blackness of the night, a steady drizzle of rain had set in. It was cold, bitterly cold; although it was but early October there was a breath of winter already in the air. The town seemed to have succumbed to the depressing effect of the cheerless day: the streets, even in the centre, were quiet, the shops closed and few people astir.'7

It was a place that was ugly, dominated by the works of man: the smoke from thirty thousand chimneys in dismal cobbled streets polluted the atmosphere, the workplaces were factories, workshops and offices. The lives of many of the inhabitants were ruled by the blare of the mill siren summoning them to work. Blackburn had been abandoned by Nature.

Contrast this description with that he wrote in his autobiography, *Ex-Fellwanderer*, published in 1987 describing his first view of Lakeland from the summit of Orrest Head in 1930. For Wainwright, it was to be a life-changing moment:

'Alighting from the bus, our first objective, according to my itinerary, was Orrest Head, a recommended viewpoint nearby. Our way led up a lane amongst lovely trees, passing large houses that seemed to me like castles, with gardens fragrant with flowers. I thought how wonderful it must be to live in a house with a garden. The sun was shining, the birds singing. We went on, climbing steadily under a canopy of foliage, the path becoming rougher, and then, quite suddenly, we emerged from the shadows of the trees and were on a bare headland, and, as though a curtain had dramatically been torn aside, beheld a truly magnificent view. It was a moment of magic, a revelation so unexpected that I stood transfixed, unable to believe my eyes. I saw mountain ranges, one after another, the nearer starkly etched, those beyond fading into the blue distance. Rich woodlands, emerald pastures and the shimmering waters of the lake below added to a pageant of loveliness, a glorious panorama that held me enthralled. I had seen landscapes of rural beauty pictured in the local art gallery, but here was no painted canvas; this was real. This was truth. God was in his heaven that day and I a humble worshipper.

The mountains compelled my attention most. They were all nameless strangers to me, although I recognised the Langdale Pikes from photographs I had seen. They looked exciting and friendly. I fancied they were beckoning me to their midst. Cloud shadows chased across them as I watched, and momentarily they appeared gloomy and frightening, but with the return of the sun they were smiling again. Come on and join us, they seemed to say.

There were no big factories and tall chimneys and crowded tenements to disfigure a scene of supreme beauty, and there was a profound stillness and tranquillity. There was no sound other than the singing of larks overhead. No other visitors came....

I felt I was some other person; this was not me. I wasn't accustomed or entitled to such a privilege. I was an alien here. I didn't belong. If only I could, sometime! If only I could! Those few hours on Orrest Head cast a spell that changed my life.'[8]

The view from Orrest Head
A Fifth Lakeland Sketchbook, No. 348

It was what he called his 'awakening to beauty'[9] and in that phrase we learn the importance of this moment in Wainwright's life. A curtain was truly torn aside as he realised that there was a world of beauty beyond the

Awakening to Beauty

grimy streets, rows of slum dwellings and wailing factory sirens. He had only seen scenes of beauty like this in paintings. But the scene before his eyes was reality. Like a doubting Thomas he declared: '. . . this was real. This was truth.' In his 1939 'autobiography', he wrote:

> 'In 1930 he went with his cousin from Yorkshire for a walking holiday in the Lake District. The beauty of the changing scenes enslaved him, but set free in his heart something that had been captive. He lived a whole lifetime during that week, a lifetime of happiness. . . .'[10]

His reaction to the beauty of the Lake District was more than the visual contrast between town and country. It was the beauty of the landscape, the serenity, and the sights and sounds of Nature that captivated his soul.

* * * * * * *

Throughout all his books, Wainwright made many references to the beauty of the landscape including references to specific natural features, particular views, weather conditions or seasonal changes. He found beauty where man worked in harmony with Nature and even rare examples where he thought man had improved on Nature.

Wainwright could find beauty in the most surprising places, such as the following occasion when returning home from his annual visit to Scotland. He was travelling back to Kendal by train from the north of Scotland when he decided to divert his journey to Stranraer hoping to find some dry weather. He described it in a letter to Molly Lefebure in May 1965:

> 'When I got to Perth, the rain it was sluicing down, so I kept on the train to Glasgow, where the rain it was sluicing down, so I changed trains for Stranraer, where the rain it was sluicing down. Stranraer, like Wick, is the end of the railway and the end of hope: the sort of place you would go to commit suicide. . . .
>
> Beauty is often glimpsed in unexpected places, and it can be found in certain conditions even at Stranraer. Looking out to the harbour from my window at bedtime, I found that the rain had stopped and a yellow band had appeared across the sky to the west, an afterglow of sunset, against which was silhouetted the

masts of the Irish steamer that had crept in during the evening and was now ablaze with lights. I looked at this pretty picture a long time. It pleased me.'[11]

Wainwright loved trees and they featured in many of his sketches. Long-established woods were honoured as places of 'sylvan beauty' or 'sylvan charm' and mature specimens were often described as 'noble' as in these examples:

'The River Greta has its beginnings in the bleak wilderness of Stainmore, whence it flows east, gradually assuming a sylvan charm as it enters the Brignall woods and becoming very beautiful in Rokeby Park, where it is confined in a rocky gorge so well wooded on both sides that the branches of trees interlace to form a canopy of foliage.'[12]

The River Greta at Rokeby
A Second Dales Sketchbook, No. 80

Càrn Eilrig (deer-trap hill)
Scottish Mountain Drawings, Volume Five,
The Eastern Highlands, No. 307

'Now partly a Nature Reserve, the great Forest of Rothiemurchus is the largest and finest surviving remnant of the original Caledonian Forest that once covered much of the Highlands and cloaks the valley south of the Spey from Loch an Eilein to Loch Morlich in a wealth of noble old pines carpeted by heather and juniper, putting to shame some conifer plantations recently interspersed. Nature has been bountiful here and the combination of lovely trees, woodland glades and cascading streams backed by colourful and craggy hillsides makes a scene of surpassing beauty. Walking in the forest on its maze of paths is a joy.'[13]

Another favoured description was to liken wooded valleys or dells to the mythical land of Arcadia, in Ancient Greek legends the domain of Pan, god of the forest, wooded areas and pastures. Eighteenth-century landscape artists featured Arcadia as an idyllic unspoilt countryside in their paintings. In *A Coast to Coast Walk*, Wainwright likened Littlebeck to a 'miniature Arcadia':

> 'The rough track indicated crosses open ground, enters a lane and is then joined by a road from Sleights for the steep descent to the hamlet of Littlebeck, a miniature Arcadia embowered in trees, a glimpse of heaven for nerve-frayed towndwellers.'[14]

Littlebeck
A Coast to Coast Walk, p. 154

Occasionally, Wainwright would write about individual trees such as the rowan tree he found on the ascent of Robinson.[15] There was also a Scots pine tree at the foot of Holme Fell that he passed frequently on his walks:

> 'If the district were without lakes and mountains it would still be very lovely because of the great wealth and variety of its trees. Most regular visitors will have their own favourite individual specimens and greet them like old friends year by year as acquaintance is renewed.
> Here, almost opposite the Hodge Close road junction, is a solitary Scots pine that the author has long admired.'[16]

A walk along a riverbank was a pleasure for Wainwright. The constant movement and sound of the water delighted the senses and the perceived beauty of the river was enhanced by knowing it provided a diverse habitat for many plants and creatures. He loved the great northern rivers: the Tyne and the Tees, in particular. His first acquaintance with both was on his Pennine Journey walk and, three decades later, he was exploring the same ground researching the route of the Pennine Way. He wrote fondly of the walk alongside the River Tees in his guidebook:

The River Tees above Middleton
Pennine Way Companion, p. 73

'And the Tees is an excellent companion: above Middleton it is a beautiful river, in places sliding smoothly in a wide bed, in places falling and cascading in rocky channels, and it has attracted to it a wealth of lovely trees, a host of darting birds and a fragrant wild flower garden along its banks. On a sunny June day, the five miles to High Force are a joy to the naturalist, the geologist and the botanist; and to the walker who has tramped the bleak moors from Edale they are perfect delight: this is a place to linger, to rest awhile in sylvan sweetness, and dream. Upper Teesdale, away from the river, has no greater charms than many places already visited, or that will be visited in the days ahead: no, it is the river, the Tees, with its bordering carpet of flowers, that enchants the eye and uplifts the heart . . . . and yet makes a man sad because, having found this Arcadia, he must leave it and may never return.'[17]

In the Lake District, the Duddon was a river that charmed Wainwright:

'The isolated buildings of Grassguards may be reached by either of two routes from the Duddon Valley. From Seathwaite church a path leads through woodlands, crossing Tarn Beck, to a bridge that has replaced stepping stones on the River Duddon in a setting joyful to behold: here the river is seen issuing from the steep confining slopes of Wallowbarrow Gorge, a ravine bedecked with heather and trees, and always a place of bewitching beauty.'[18]

The Duddon at Wallowbarrow
A Second Furness Sketchbook, No. 58

Changing weather conditions as well as seasonal variations brought a transient beauty to the landscape, transforming familiar scenes into spectacles of magical splendour. Sunlight and shadows could bring drama to a landscape together with the effects of moving clouds creating constant changes in the lighting, adding its own beauty to the scene. Whilst on his 1938 Pennine Journey, Wainwright described the effects of changing light on a heather-clad moor:

> 'Yet it was not the immensity of this moor that made it dominant in the landscape I saw. It was the heather. I had not seen the glory of heather until today. It was the heather that gave the colour to the picture; a gorgeous crimson-purple, dark where the shadows chased across it, bright in the sunlight. Every slope and undulation carried its own banner of warm colour.'[19]

Being a warm morning, he lay down on his heather bed to contemplate the passing clouds:

> 'There was no breeze on the moor, but overhead white clouds were drifting quickly across the blue dome of heaven. I watched them come, stealing silently out of the west, squadron after squadron; witnessed their solemn procession above my head; saw them dissolve into the mist to the east. Big clouds and little clouds, there were; stately schooners in full rig, travelling in slow majesty; tiny yachts with wispy sails, speeding quickly to overtake the others, eager to make a race of it. I lay there, stretched out in the heather, and reviewed the fleet.
>
> Clouds are the most transient of nature's creations. They come out of a clear sky, disintegrate before your eyes, vanish. You never see the same cloud twice. Every moment of its brief existence brings a change, a change of form or tint or texture; but its beauty remains constant to the end. The beauty of the clouds is there for us to see every day, if we are not too busy to look up, but if they peep at us over grimy buildings we shall not appreciate their grandeur so well. Seen from a mountain side, they have never the dull, leaden effect which often characterises their appearance when they overhang the towns; they are never grey, never shapeless, never lustreless. Best of all is to look at clouds from above. Look down on them, not up at them; climb through them

to Gable's summit on a wet day, and stand there in brilliant sunshine, looking across to Scafell or Pillar, rocky islands in a sea of billowing white. You will love clouds thereafter, be they ever so bleak and forbidding. For from above, they are always white, pure white. And always very beautiful.'[20]

Seasonal changes brought their own unique beauty to the landscape, particularly in autumn and winter. Autumn in the Lake District is beautiful, but following his divorce in 1968, Wainwright asked Betty if she would like to holiday in Scotland that October. He had never visited so late in the year and the autumn colours in the glens enthralled him. In his letters he described the magnificent scenes he had witnessed.

Ben Tee and Sron a' Choire Ghairbh overlooking Glen Garry
Scottish Mountain Drawings, Volume Two,
The North-Western Highlands, No. 143

To Molly Lefebure:
'I had a wonderful holiday in Scotland, the best ever. . . . After the mild summer, the leaves were still on the trees, making a most gorgeous riot of yellows and reds and bronzes. I withdraw what I

Awakening to Beauty

have said before, that Lakeland is lovelier than the Highlands of Scotland. It isn't. In fact, after seeing the Scottish glens in autumn, it beats me why people rave about the Lake District.'[21]

To Mr Hancock (in reply to a fan letter):
 'Scotland is magnificent (north of Glasgow) but I have never conceded that it is more beautiful than Lakeland – until last October, when I got a late chance to make yet another tour by car, and, not having been up there so late in the year before, was absolutely spellbound by the glorious autumn colours. Loch Lomond, in sunshine, was a dream of delight, the birches in Glen Garry showed a beauty out of this world, Loch Maree was a fairyland. The whole place was lit up by colours I had not suspected from summer visits. I was enthralled.'[22]

Another favoured season for Wainwright was winter when the summer visitors had departed and the fells and valleys were, once again, havens of peace. It was then that snow could transform the fells into a winter wonderland:

Skiddaw, from Friar's Crag
A Fifth Lakeland Sketchbook, No. 391

'Visitors to the Lakes are lovers of beauty yet most never see the district in its winter raiment, when the valleys are transformed by snow into a fairyland of glittering crystals and the fells seemingly add to their stature and stand gaunt and aloof in white mantles. This is a new beauty and not a lesser one.'[23]

He remembered one particular winter in the 1960s:

'The other season I recall vividly was the winter of 1963-4. The district was gripped by a severe frost for three months without respite, the lakes were sheets of ice and the fells encased in frozen snow. The conditions put paid to fellwalking. But the scenery of the valleys was very beautiful. Borrowdale, which I visited each Sunday, was transformed into a fairyland of exquisite charm, a delicate tracery of black and white. I was entranced. This was a new Lakeland. Even without colour it was the loveliest place on earth.'[24]

Tarn Hows, in the Lake District, was created by raising the water level of natural pools in a marshy hollow that, with the addition of extensive tree planting, has matured into a landscape of great beauty that Wainwright called: 'a rare example of man improving on nature':[25]

Tarn Hows, looking northeast
A Furness Sketchbook, No. 15

'The picture that greets the eye on arriving at the outflow is as pretty as can be imagined: a delightful lake with many bays and inlets has been created by the merging of three small natural tarns artificially, the scene being set in a framework of trees and presided over by Black Fell in the background. For once, and unusually, man has rivalled nature as a bewitching landscape artist. . . . Fortunate indeed is the visitor who prefers to contemplate beauty undisturbed and finds himself alone at Tarn Hows'.[26]

Wainwright was inspired by natural beauty wherever he found it: on Orrest Head in 1930, the sylvan beauty of a Scottish glen in autumn, the tumbling cascades of a northern river or snow-covered mountains in the Lake District. Through his experiences, Wainwright had discovered that an appreciation of beauty in Nature was good for the soul and could bring peace and happiness to a troubled heart.

NOTES

[1] The full title of the poem is: *Lines Composed a Few Miles above Tintern Abbey, on Revisiting the Banks of the Wye during a Tour, July 13, 1798*

[2] William Wordsworth, *Lyrical Ballads with a Few Other Poems*, 1798, pp. 201-2 Lines 1-8

[3] William Wordsworth, *Lyrical Ballads with a Few Other Poems*, 1798, pp. 202-4, Lines 25-33 & Lines 59-61

[4] William Wordsworth, *Lyrical Ballads with a Few Other Poems*, 1798, pp. 207-9, Lines 106-111 & Lines 127-139
Text of *Lines Composed a Few Miles above Tintern Abbey*, see website: https://en.wikisource.org/wiki/Page:Lyrical_Ballads_(Coleridge).djvu/221

[5] *The Wainwright Letters*, edited by Hunter Davies, p. 50

[6] The 'autobiography' was written in the third person referring to himself as Michael Wayne. In interviews, Wainwright said that he disliked the name 'Alfred'.

[7] *Wainwright's unpublished story manuscript*, 1939
MS held at the Kendal Archive Centre, WDAW/1/24/1 pp. 1&2

[8] *Ex-Fellwanderer*, unpaginated

[9] *The Outlying Fells of Lakeland*, p. 26

[10] *Wainwright's unpublished story manuscript*, 1939
MS held at the Kendal Archive Centre, WDAW/1/24/1 pp. 29&30

[11] *The Wainwright Letters*, edited by Hunter Davies, p. 143

[12] *A Second Dales Sketchbook*, No. 80

[13] *Wainwright in Scotland*, pp. 190-1

A Newt in Hard Tarn

---

[14] *A Coast to Coast Walk*, p. 154
[15] For the full story, *see*: *The North Western Fells*, Robinson p. 8
[16] *The Southern Fells*, Holme Fell p. 2
[17] *Pennine Way Companion*, p. 74
[18] *Wainwright on the Lakeland Mountain Passes*, p. 71
[19] *A Pennine Journey*, p. 77
[20] *A Pennine Journey*, pp. 77-8
[21] *The Wainwright Letters*, edited by Hunter Davies, p. 230
[22] *The Wainwright Letters*, edited by Hunter Davies, p. 246
[23] *A Fifth Lakeland Sketchbook*, No. 391
[24] *Ex-Fellwanderer*, unpaginated
[25] *A Lakeland Sketchbook*, No. 60
[26] *Wainwright in the Valleys of Lakeland*, p. 94

CHAPTER FIVE

Nature's Designs

Nature lay at the centre of Romantic philosophy and was a guiding light for the early Romantic poets. Nature was the physical manifestation of God's Word and by communing with Nature it was possible to come to a better awareness and understanding of God's divine purposes. Coleridge expounded this philosophy in his poem, *Frost at Midnight*, written in 1798. His own father had died when he was nine years old and he was sent up to London from his childhood home in Devon to complete his education at a charity school. It was an experience he never forgot and he was determined to bring up his own son, Hartley, as a child of Nature. In the poem he recalls his own childhood in London and how Hartley's life will be different by living close to Nature and through this experience he will come to an awareness of God's divine plan for his life:

> 'For I was reared
> In the great city, pent mid cloisters dim,
> And saw nought lovely but the sky and stars.
> But *thou*, my babe! Shalt wander, like a breeze,
> By lakes and sandy shores, beneath the crags
> Of ancient mountain, and beneath the clouds,
> Which image in their bulk both lakes and shores
> And mountain crags: so shalt thou see and hear
> The lovely shapes and sounds intelligible
> Of that eternal language, which thy God
> Utters, who from eternity doth teach
> Himself in all, and all things in himself.
> Great universal Teacher! he shall mould
> Thy spirit, and by giving make it ask.'[1]

Wordsworth linked Nature to God's purposes in a more understated way in his poem, *Lines Composed a Few Miles above Tintern Abbey* (discussed in the preceding chapter: *see* pp. 35-7). He writes about feeling: 'the joy of elevated thoughts' and the presence of God in the natural world: air, sea, sky and the light of the setting sun:

> 'And I have felt
> A presence that disturbs me with the joy
> Of elevated thoughts; a sense sublime
> Of something far more deeply interfused,
> Whose dwelling is the light of setting suns,
> And the round ocean and the living air,
> And the blue sky, and in the mind of man:
> A motion and a spirit, that impels
> All thinking things, all objects of all thought,
> And rolls through all things.'[2]

Wordsworth understood there was a link between Nature and man that guided his thoughts and actions. Put simply, Nature was his moral compass:

> 'In nature and the language of the sense
> The anchor of my purest thoughts, the nurse,
> The guide, the guardian of my heart, and soul
> Of all my moral being.'[3]

* * * * * * *

Wainwright was probably more Wordsworthian in his thinking about God and Nature. As a child in Blackburn, the family attended the local chapel and he continued to do so into early adulthood. But by the close of the 1920s he was finding little spiritual benefit from attending the weekly services. He admitted in *Ex-Fellwanderer* that his attendance was more to please his mother than for any other reason:

> 'I was totally absorbed by my studies in the later part of the 1920s and went into a shell, having no time for my old acquaintances and very little for my family apart from my mother. To please her I continued to attend the chapel each week but gained no spiritual uplift from these visits, was bored and sceptical of religious teachings.'[4]

Nature's Designs

However, his holiday to the Lake District in 1930 had changed him. He had discovered true happiness and peace of mind in the beauty of the natural world and in climbing mountains he felt the presence of God in a way that he had never done in a church:

> 'On a hill I am alone, and sincere; anywhere else, I am one of a crowd and tinged with mob instincts of selfishness and hypocrisy. Yet it is neither the sight of a hill nor the feel of it beneath me that brings the transformation, for transformation it is; rather it is that in the high places I am very conscious of the nearness of God; so aware of His presence all about me that I could never feel lonely. But if I am in a church in the valley, I am lost: I cannot feel the same, try as I will.'[5]

He wrote this in 1939 in his first book (*A Pennine Journey*) and by 1941 he had stopped attending services at the chapel in Blackburn. But he had not rejected God completely as this letter demonstrates, sent to Eric Maudsley the following year:

> 'A few hours spent in contemplation and meditation above the cliffs of Scafell, in silent worship at the cathedral of the Pinnacle, does more for a man's soul than a thousand sermons. Could you sit there and call yourself an atheist, an unbeliever? I do not think so for a moment; your doubts must surely have been lost in the gulf of Mickledore, swept away by the clean winds.'[6]

Once he had moved to Kendal and had the Lake District on his doorstep, Nature became his inspiration and, like Wordsworth, became the touchstone of his beliefs, 'the guardian of [his] heart and soul'. He acknowledged a Creator, but Nature had its own natural force and power. Consider what he wrote about standing on the ridge of Mickledore less than twenty years after his letter to Eric Maudsley, this written in *The Southern Fells* in 1959:

> 'A man may stand on the lofty ridge of Mickledore, or in the green hollow beneath the precipice amongst the littered debris and boulders fallen from it, and witness the sublime architecture of the buttresses and pinnacles soaring into the sky, silhouetted against racing clouds or, often, tormented by writhing mists, and,

as in a great cathedral, lose all his conceit. It does a man good to realise his own insignificance in the general scheme of things and that is his experience here.'[7]

It is a natural landscape – rocks, crags, threatening clouds and mist – that arouses awe and wonder as if one was inside a cathedral. But this is Nature's cathedral, not made by man for the worship of God, and, for Wainwright, invoked a similar spiritual experience.

Scafell Crag and Mickledore, from Lingmell
A Fourth Lakeland Sketchbook, No. 297

Nature could also unleash its destructive power as Wainwright noted when writing his chapter about Lingmell in *The Southern Fells*. Violent storms caused huge quantities of rock, boulders and scree to be carried down Lingmell's two becks, wreaking havoc on the little community at Wasdale Head and covering the valley pastures with rock and other detritus:

'Lingmell Beck and Lingmell Gill are its streams, both flowing into Wast Water in wide channels and boulder-choked courses, testimony to the fury of the storms and cloudbursts that have riven the fellsides in past years; there is, indeed, a vast area of denudation (Lingmell Scars) on the slope overlooking Brown Tongue, and the devastated lakeside fields below Brackenclose add their witness to the power of the floods that have carried the debris down to the valley.'[8]

Nature in the raw was demonstrated by the power of the sea and its effects on the coastline. Wainwright visited Cape Wrath, at the northwest tip of mainland Scotland, only once. He was taken there by the film crew in his Scottish film series in 1987. As they gazed at the endless waves pounding the base of the granite headland, Eric Robson asked: 'Well, it's taken you eighty-odd years to get here. Worth the trip?' Wainwright replied prosaically: 'I'm glad I've seen it.'[9] But when *Wainwright in Scotland* was published, he wrote with feeling:

'Cape Wrath, the most northerly point of Sutherland, is well named. Nature is in an angry mood here. The Atlantic has waged an unceasing war against this gaunt headland ever since the beginning of time, hurling its waves in fury at the unyielding rocks without respite; there is always the noise of thrashing waters. This is the wildest place in Britain, primitive, raw and undisciplined, with the lighthouse, built in 1848, the only evidence of the intrusion of man. The towering cliffs, rising to a vertical 350 feet below the lighthouse and to 800 feet in places to the east, are the highest in mainland Britain and are virgin, just as they were sculptured, and explored only by the countless seabirds to which they are home. The scenery inspires awe and apprehension and fear even on a summer day; in stormy conditions, the effect is frightening.'[10]

* * * * * * *

As well as the power to inspire awe, wonder, apprehension and fear, there was a belief that Nature had the capacity to heal and soothe. The healing power of Nature was a central tenet of the Romantic poets. It was accepted that Nature could soothe the troubled mind or spirit and had the power to quell sudden fear or pain.

As an example of the latter was an incident, recorded by Coleridge in his Notebook, when his infant son, Hartley, had fallen and hurt himself.

Coleridge's reaction was to gather up his son, who was crying, and take him outside where he was calmed almost immediately by the sight of the Moon shining in the night sky.

The following year, Coleridge incorporated the story into his poem, *The Nightingale*. He was making the point that in the past the song of the nightingale was thought to be sad, inducing feelings of melancholy. But, for Coleridge, it was a joyful, natural sound that could bring joy to the listener, just as the Moon at night had soothed and calmed his son.

Many times in his writing, Wainwright referred to his sense of peace and tranquillity of mind and spirit when walking alone on the hills. In his book, *A Pennine Journey*, Wainwright contrasts the calming effects engendered by a walk in a natural landscape of hills, with urban living:

> 'Oh, how can I put into words the joys of a walk over country such as this; the scenes that delight the eyes, the blessed peace of mind, the sheer exuberance which fills your soul as you tread the firm turf? This is something to be lived, not read about. On these breezy heights, a transformation is wondrously wrought within you. Your thoughts are simple, in tune with your surroundings; the complicated problems you brought with you from the town are smoothed away. . . . Something happens to you in the silent places which never could in the towns, and it is a good thing to sit awhile in a quiet spot and meditate. The hills have a power to soothe and heal which is their very own.'[11]

On Grange Fell, in the Lake District, Wainwright perceived that Nature provided the perfect setting, enabling a solitary walker to reconnect with natural beauty and refresh and revitalise the soul. Communing with Nature on the quieter fells brought peace and serenity to a troubled mind:

> 'Grange Fell is nothing on the map, everything when beneath one's feet. In small compass, here is concentrated the beauty, romance, interest and excitement of the typical Lakeland scene. Here Nature has given of her very best and produced a loveliness that is exquisite. Not strictly the territory of fellwalkers, perhaps; yet those who consistently hurry past Grange Fell to get to grips with the Scafells and Gable would do well to turn aside to it once in a while, alone, and quietly walk its sylvan glades and heathery

Nature's Designs

top. The exercise will not tire the limbs, but it will do the heart and spirit and faith of the walker a power of good, and gladden his eye exceedingly.'[12]

Kings How, Grange Fell
The Central Fells, Grange Fell, p. 1

* * * * * * *

Wainwright was fascinated by the bewildering variety of upland landscapes that he encountered on his walks. These were Nature's designs, all unique and all capable of eliciting differing emotions: awe, wonder, fear, joy, astonishment and even amusement.

He never revealed which mountain in the Lake District was his favourite. In his Pictorial Guides he listed six at the end of Book 7 (*The Western Fells*). All but Blencathra were in the volcanic south-western sector, but this was the mountain that formed the longest chapter in the book series. He lavished three pages on the description of the southern front, a natural wonder of design and what he called: 'a remarkable example of the effect of elemental natural forces.'[13]

He acknowledges Nature as the 'master architect' of what he describes as: 'one of the grandest objects in Lakeland':[14]

> 'The outer slopes, rising on the west and east flanks from valley level to the uppermost escarpment below the summit ridge, are smoothly curved, massive and yet so symmetrical that they might well have been designed by a master architect to supply a perfect balance to the structure.'[15]

Out of the seeming chaos of a primeval collapse, Nature has restored order and balance in its design:

> 'The picture is chaotic: a great upheaval of ridges and pinnacles rising out of dead wastes of scree and penetrated by choked gullies and ravines, the whole crazily tilted through 2000' of altitude. Even in this area of confusion and disorder, however, Nature has sculptured a distinct pattern.
> Four watercourses emerge from surrounding debris to escape to the valley.
> Between the four ravines, three lofty spurs alike in main characteristics, thrust far out; narrow and frail where they leave the solid mass of the mountain, they widen into substantial buttresses as they descend to the valley. It is as though a giant hand had clawed at the mountain, each finger scooping out a deep hollow, with narrow strips of ground left undisturbed between.'[16]

But seen from valley level, the effect of the steep rocky buttresses and intervening gills on the emotions is one of awe and even fear:

> 'It forms a tremendous facade above the valley, and makes a dark, towering backcloth to a stage of farmsteads and cottages, of emerald pastures and meadows and woodlands along its base. There is nothing inviting in these shattered cliffs and petrified rivers of stone that seem to hold a perpetual threat over the little community below: the scene arrests attention, but intimidates and repels. Few who gaze upon these desolate walls are likely to feel any inclination and inspiration to scramble up through their arid, stony wildernesses to the contorted skyline so high above.'[17]

Nature's Designs

Blencathra, from St. John's Vale
A Lakeland Sketchbook, No. 54

Natural piling of rocks could produce weird and wonderful effects. Wainwright took the photograph for this sketch on his first holiday to Scotland in 1939, visiting the island of Arran. He wrote:

> 'Illustrated is a striking example of rock architecture on Beinn Tarsuinn (although one suspects that the 'eye' has been added by human agency).'[18]

A granite tor, Beinn Tarsuinn
Scottish Mountain Drawings, Volume Six, The Islands, No. 450

Brimham Rocks is an example of natural weathering that Wainwright called: 'a world of fantasy'. He must have enjoyed drawing these sketches:

> 'There is no other place in the country like Brimham Rocks, where ages of wind and rain and frost have carved the most grotesque and fantastic shapes out of a desert of exposed gritstone. Here are Nature's sculptures in amazing variety and profusion – sixty acres of moorland littered with rocks that bear an uncanny resemblance to animals, that tower as slender monoliths, that stand precariously balanced on others. . . . This is an astonishing place, almost beyond belief. Here one passes from the world of reality to a world of fantasy.'[19]

Brimham Rocks
A Dales Sketchbook, No. 52

No further explanation is needed for this sketch of the Wain Stones at Bleaklow Head on the Pennine Way, with Wainwright's whimsical caption.

The Wain Stones
Pennine Way Companion, p. 162

Wainwright was well aware that most upland landscapes were managed and changed by human intervention – man and Nature working together could improve the landscape.

In the Lake District it was the partnership between man and Nature that created a landscape that Wainwright described as romantic charm and he was ready to praise these efforts where the result was beneficial. In his final book, he looked back nostalgically to the 1930s when he made his first visits to Langdale and recalled the idyllic scenery that had been created by the first dalesmen working in harmony with Nature to tame and improve the wild valley:

Great Langdale
Fellwanderer

'When Nature completed her masterly landscape architecture ages ago and later the early dalesmen smoothed the rough places and furbished them with rich pastures and woodlands, then indeed there was distinction, rare and flawless, in the scenery thus created. Time was, within living memory, that a walker could wander all day in Langdale and enjoy undisturbed peace with the songs of birds and the murmur of waters as a musical accompaniment; he would meet only a few others, and they of like mind, intent on quiet appreciation of the wonderful surroundings. We walked in fairyland. A solitary bus took us into the valley from Ambleside in the mornings and came back for us in the evenings. Those were halcyon days, gone, never to return.'[20]

When Wainwright was researching the route of the Pennine Way, he encountered empty moorland landscapes where there was very little evidence of the hand of man. These desolate landscapes were very different to areas that had been despoiled by human activity such as military use, forestry or the flooding of valleys for water supply. This, Wainwright called devastation. He distinguished the two like this:

> 'Desolation and Devastation
> A scene of desolation can be very beautiful; a scene of devastation is always downright ugly. Nature fashions desolation; man causes devastation. Nature's wildernesses often have charm; man's wildernesses are without charm. . . . Nature creates; man destroys.'[21]

Wainwright believed that Nature was under attack and he felt compelled to criticise the authorities where he perceived these threats to the natural world.

He loved trees and was angered when they were planted commercially in serried ranks with no room to breathe and grow naturally. He likened it to battery farming and felt only sadness for these poor specimens fighting for their existence. One example was in Wark Forest on the route of the Pennine Way:

> 'Nobody loves trees more than I do, but for these wretched spruces there can only be compassion. Down in the forest nothing stirs. There is no bird song. There is silence and the atmosphere of a graveyard. One feels sorry for these densely-packed trees, not one growing as it would wish and living the miserable existence of battery hens. Every tree starts life wanting to be a noble and beautiful specimen, but these poor things are deliberately starved of sunlight even from birth. Except around the fringes of the forest they are skeletons, without foliage, their branches withered, barely surviving in the darkness of a tomb, the intention of the planters being that they should grow tall as they fight for air and light, and so develop a commercial value. They grow, not as trees but as poles. This is man's design, not nature's. It is always man that commits the affronts to a natural and fulfilled existence, of animals as well as trees. He is top dog in this world, and don't you forget it.'[22]

Nature's Designs

But when Nature was left alone, even in the midst of desolation, Wainwright was uplifted by the rare beauty that was created in landscapes that would repel many for the reasons that attracted him: the silence and solitude. Rannoch Moor in the Scottish Highlands was one such place:

Rannoch Moor, looking towards Meall Buidhe (yellow rounded hill)
Scottish Mountain Drawings, Volume Four,
The Central Highlands, No. 266

'Rannoch Moor is a desolation fashioned by Nature and right well has she succeeded. A thousand feet above sea level and sixty square miles in extent, the moor is a vast tableland, so flat that it appears at first sight to be ideal terrain for walking. It is nothing of the sort, found on close acquaintance to be a labyrinth of bogs, pools, lochans and lochs, stagnant watercourses unable to decide which way to go, and squelching morasses....

I never tire of Rannoch Moor. It always gives me pleasure in any conditions, sunlit or under brooding cloud: the silence, the solitude, the panoramas of distant mountains etched against the sky in all directions, the resident deer, the heather, the bog myrtle, all contribute a charm to this no-man's-land. Here is desolation with a subtle beauty.'[23]

* * * * * * *

Another device used by Wainwright was to give Nature a voice, bestowing it with human characteristics – the ability to think and speak and express emotions.

This was a literary device used by the Romantic poets, often to contrast the goodness of Nature with the more questionable affairs of man. In his poem, *Lines Written in Early Spring*, Wordsworth compares the thoughts of pleasure he experiences when observing Nature around him – the flowers, birds and trees – with his sad thoughts when he thinks of how society has changed in recent times. The French Revolution had brought misery to many in France and was influencing events in Britain.

In the poem, winter is over and Nature is revelling in the warmth and longer days of spring. Nature is personified by having the same capacity as humans for thought and enjoyment. The flowers enjoy breathing the fresh, clean air, the birds take pleasure in playing and the budding twigs on the trees appreciate the warmer winds. While Nature brings joy to the poet, he feels only sadness when he thinks of the deeds of man:

> 'Through primrose tufts, in that green bower,
> The periwinkle trail'd its wreathes;
> And 'tis my faith that every flower
> Enjoys the air it breathes.
>
> The birds around me hopp'd and play'd,
> Their thoughts I cannot measure,
> But the least motion which they made,
> It seem'd a thrill of pleasure.
>
> The budding twigs spread out their fan,
> To catch the breezy air;
> And I must think, do all I can,
> That there was pleasure there.
>
> If I these thoughts may not prevent,
> If such be of my creed the plan,
> Have I not reason to lament
> What man has made of man?'[24]

Nature's Designs

Wainwright's use of the personification of Nature is primarily to express opinions about unnecessary or harmful human development of the landscape. In particular, he highlights exploitation of upland landscapes, urbanisation of the countryside and the development of industrial sites.

When writing *The Northern Fells* he described Skiddaw as being the head of a family with seven children, the view from the south looking rather like a family photograph:

> 'There is a classical quality about this view from the south. Skiddaw and its outliers rise magnificently across the wide Vale of Keswick in a beautifully-symmetrical arrangement, as if posed for a family photograph. The old man himself is the central figure at the back of the group, with his five older children in a line before him (the favourite son, Little Man, being placed nearest) and the two younger children at the front.'[25]

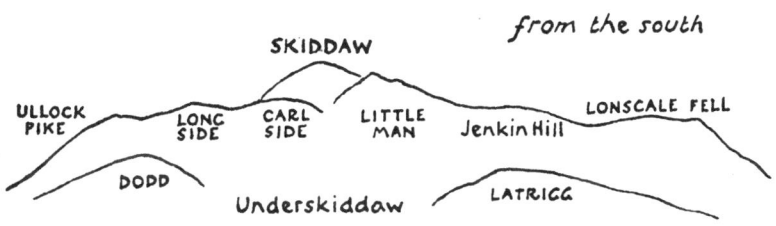

The Skiddaw range, from the south
The Northern Fells, Skiddaw, p. 4

However, all is not well in the family, as Wainwright explained. Dodd is the odd man out, a whelp that Skiddaw has thought to disown because of a recent planting of 'foreign' trees by the Forestry Commission. Skiddaw is not amused and exclaims, grumpily: 'Bah!'

> 'Dodd, like Latrigg, can be described as a whelp of Skiddaw crouched at the feet of his parent. But Dodd has latterly shown nothing of the family characteristics and the old man must today regard his offspring with surprise and growing doubt, and feel like denying his paternity and disowning the little wretch....
> In years gone by Dodd sported few small woodlands, like a young man his first moustaches, with such success and evidence

A Newt in Hard Tarn

of fertility as to attract the attention of the Forestry Commission, then developing the Thornthwaite Forest just across Bassenthwaite Lake. Since 1920 the Commission have been rampant here, and, except for a single field at Little Crosthwaite, they have covered the fell thickly with growing timber....

Skiddaw's frown betrays an old prejudice; true, Skiddaw has long had his own Forest but *that* is fine rolling upland country not desecrated by fancy trees . . . . . *foreign* trees, moreover! If there *must* be trees on Dodd, aren't Lakeland trees good enough? Bah! says Skiddaw.'[26]

The summit of Dodd
The Northern Fells, Dodd, p. 12

Wainwright's objection was the fact that they were not native trees, which would look right in the Lakeland landscape. No doubt he would be pleased to learn that the trees were felled some years ago restoring the beautiful view he could see only by standing on tiptoes:

'This is the weirdest of all summits, a place to visit – and flee from. The old cairn is there, as it was when the hilltop was grass pasture but in the course of the years it has been insidiously overshadowed by a new and taller growth: a few hundred specimens of *Pinus mugo*, the mountain pine. This unsightly tree, of a strange and ghostly appearance, now covers the top completely, though a tiny clearing has been left in deference to the cairn. It is obviously not a natural adornment of Dodd, because nature does not grow her trees at regularly-spaced intervals, as these are; but it would seem to a layman that the planting has not been successful. Few of the trees are flourishing: the majority look unhealthy and even diseased and dying.'[27]

'By standing on tiptoes, craning the neck, leaping in the air and miscellaneous gyrations of the body not normally indulged in by people in their right senses it is just possible, on a clear day, to see all the fells indicated on the diagram. The obstruction is caused by *Pinus mugo*, the gaunt bare branches of which form an unbroken screen up to ten feet high all round the cairn. This is unfortunate, because enough can be seen, with difficulty to suggest that the view south, if uninterrupted, would be simply glorious.'[28]

In his later years, Wainwright drew a series of sketchbooks of his local rivers in Cumbria, the Dales and north Lancashire. Rivers were born to run free but all had been harnessed by man for work and, in places, their natural beauty was threatened by industrialisation and urbanisation. Wainwright imagined rivers as living entities being born in the hills, coming to maturity in middle age before finally dying and being buried in the alien waters of the sea. Rivers had feelings and emotions and in this series of books he gave them a voice to express their feelings about their treatment by the hand of man.

His first book was *Three Westmorland Rivers*, the Mint and the Sprint both flowing into the River Kent that flowed though his home town of Kendal. It saddened him to see the treatment of these three beautiful rivers, so lovely in early life, so carefree, only to be abused in maturity:

'If rivers have feelings, the Mint must be sad indeed as it passes under the Shap road and, in dismay, is confronted by a huge

A Newt in Hard Tarn

complex of factory buildings. It is an honour, of course, to have the last of its bridges named after it, but poor compensation for the drabness of these foreign surroundings in which its life must end. O for the hills of Bannisdale, the trees of Shaw End, the serenity of Rossill and Laverock! There was beauty in those places, but here is squalor and ugliness and noise: no fit setting for a requiem. The mingling of its waters with those of the Kent should be a happy rendezvous, but it is not. How could it be, with Bannisdale still fresh in mind?'[29]

Watersmeet, Mint and Kent
Three Westmorland Rivers, No. 16

Of the three rivers, the Sprint was the least to suffer despoliation, retaining its charm and exuberance throughout its short life:

'The Sprint is Longsleddale's river, a joyful stream in infancy, less turbulent in maturity.'[30]

'The Sprint is at its loveliest in the vicinity of Oakbank, where, in spite of the decaying evidences of man's attempts to tame its flow, the river assumes an air of majesty as it sweeps in graceful curves through natural woodlands. Yet even here there are occasional reminders that it has not quite lost the impetuosity of its youth and sparkling cascades light up the dark surround of foliage.'[31]

The Sprint at Oakbank
Three Westmorland Rivers, No. 32

The Kent is born in a landscape of loveliness, but when it reaches Kendal its beauty has gone, industrial buildings lining its banks and flood defences having been constructed:

'It travels a journey of delight, of strong contrasts alike only in loveliness, and, because its waters leap and dance as they go, there is melody and harmony all the way.'[32]

'Soon after leaving Burneside the Kent is joined by the Sprint and a mile further by the Mint. Then Kendal is entered and the environment changes. Now for two miles there are buildings, traffic, smoke and noise – features alien and unwelcome to a river born in lonely hills and matured in green fields and woods. The

Kent in Kendal has been robbed of charm and character by unsympathetic flood-prevention "improvements" and transformed into a wide canal. And unfeeling people treat it as a drain to carry away their rubbish. Poor reward for a proud river that gave its name to the town!'[33]

The end is filled with sadness, the river finally lost in the waters of Morecambe Bay:

'Now the Kent turns westerly towards the open sea, where it is fated to drown. It is no longer happy. The sparkle has gone from it. The estuary is strange, the rush of foreign waters, dirty and evil-tasting is frightening: their noise is a lament. Where now are the trees that caressed the river and shadowed its course down the valley? Where now are the hills, the beloved mountains where it ran free? If only it could turn back and see dear Kentmere again!'[34]

Kent Estuary
Three Westmorland Rivers, No. 75

'The Kent keeps its proud name far out from land, being known as Kent Channel while yet visible at low tide. Then, as the estuary widens into the sea, its identity is lost, its mission fulfilled, its duty done, and it merges into the oblivion of Morecambe Bay.'[35]

The world of Nature with its infinite beauty was at the core of Wainwright's writing and drawing for over fifty years. Much of his leisure time was spent in solitary walking, absorbing the atmosphere and developing an affinity with the landscape and its flora and fauna that were part of the natural world.

It was love of these beautiful landscapes that inspired him to write and draw. It was the emotion he felt deep inside his soul that he wanted to convey to others, emotions that he confessed he often found difficult to articulate in mere words.

But, for the reader, his love for these landscapes shines through all his work, a love that inspires others to follow in his footsteps and share in the joy of natural beauty.

NOTES

[1] Samuel Taylor Coleridge, *Fears in Solitude, written in 1798, during the Alarm of an Invasion. to which are added, France, an Ode; and Frost at Midnight*, 1798, p. 22, Lines 56-69
Text of *Frost at Midnight, see* website: https://en.wikisource.org/wiki/Page:Fears_in_Solitude_-_Coleridge_(1798).djvu/27

[2] William Wordsworth, *Lyrical Ballads with a Few Other Poems*, 1798, p. 207, Lines 97-106

[3] William Wordsworth, *Lyrical Ballads with a Few Other Poems*, 1798, p. 208, Lines 112-115
Text of *Lines Composed a Few Miles above Tintern Abbey, see* website: https://en.wikisource.org/wiki/Page:Lyrical_Ballads_(Coleridge).djvu/221

[4] *Ex-Fellwanderer*, unpaginated

[5] *A Pennine Journey*, p. 199

[6] *The Wainwright Letters*, edited by Hunter Davies, p. 61

[7] *The Southern Fells*, Scafell p. 2

[8] *The Southern Fells*, Lingmell p. 2

[9] *Wainwright's Highlands & Islands*, BBC Worldwide Ltd., 2003, Programme 1, The Far North (first screened in 1988)

[10] *Wainwright in Scotland*, p. 17

[11] *A Pennine Journey*, pp. 30-1

[12] *The Central Fells*, Grange Fell p. 1

[13] *The Northern Fells*, Blencathra p. 3

[14] *The Northern Fells*, Blencathra p. 1

[15] *The Northern Fells*, Blencathra p. 3

[16] *The Northern Fells*, Blencathra p. 4

[17] *The Northern Fells*, Blencathra p. 3

[18] *Scottish Mountain Drawings, Volume Six, The Islands*, No. 450

[19] *A Dales Sketchbook*, No. 52

[20] *Wainwright in the Valleys of Lakeland*, p. 178

[21] *Pennine Way Companion*, p. 84

[22] *Wainwright on the Pennine Way*, p. 171

[23] *Wainwright in Scotland*, p. 139

[24] William Wordsworth, *Lyrical Ballads with a Few Other Poems*, 1798, p. 116, Lines 9-24 Text of *Lines Written In Early Spring, see* website: https://en.wikisource.org/wiki/Page:Lyrical_Ballads_(Coleridge).djvu/135

[25] *The Northern Fells*, Skiddaw p. 4

[26] *The Northern Fells*, Dodd pp. 2-3

[27] *The Northern Fells*, Dodd p. 12

[28] *The Northern Fells*, Dodd p. 14

[29] *Three Westmorland Rivers*, No. 16

[30] *Three Westmorland Rivers*, The River Sprint, Introduction

[31] *Three Westmorland Rivers*, No. 32

[32] *Three Westmorland Rivers*, The River Kent, Introduction

[33] *Three Westmorland Rivers*, No. 57

[34] *Three Westmorland Rivers*, No. 73

[35] *Three Westmorland Rivers*, No. 75

CHAPTER SIX

Emotional Revelations

In January 1803, Coleridge wrote to his friend and benefactor, Thomas Wedgwood, about a journey from Patterdale to Grasmere by way of Kirkstone Pass. At the top of the Pass he encountered stormy conditions with lashing wind and rain. It was so bad that he sent his wife, Sara, back to Patterdale:

In his reply, Thomas asked him why he had not turned back with his wife. His answer was that he did not exercise prudence when considering turning back in poor weather. As he said in his letter: 'the thought never once entered my head.'[1]

Looking down to Kirkstone Pass from Red Screes
Westmorland Heritage, p. 449

What followed was an emotional response to fellwalking, alone in the high places where he was at one with the landscape and his feelings were of intense life flowing through his body. It was as if he was immortal, indestructible. He compared himself to a chamois-chaser, an Alpine hunter of the chamois who would stalk his prey over the rockiest and most dangerous of ground with no fear of death:

* * * * * * *

Wainwright was more circumspect in his feelings but his response was no less emotional. Fellwalking was a release; an escape from the everyday world of disappointments in his personal life. He was climbing to a place where he found true peace of mind, a place of happiness – his own heaven on earth.

In the natural world, the hills symbolised truth and goodness. This emotional journey had begun in 1930 with his first visit to Lakeland and its culmination was in writing the Pictorial Guides:

> 'I suppose it might be said, to add impressiveness to the whole thing, that this book has been twenty years in the making, for it is so long, and more, since I first came from a smoky mill-town (forgive me, Blackburn!) and beheld, from Orrest Head, a scene of great loveliness, a fascinating paradise, Lakeland's mountains and trees and water. That was the first time I had looked upon beauty or imagined it, even. Afterwards I went often, whenever I could, and always my eyes were lifted to the hills. I was to find then, and it has been so ever since, a spiritual and physical satisfaction in climbing mountains – and a tranquil mind upon reaching their summits, as though I had escaped from the disappointments and unkindnesses of life and emerged above them into a new world, a better world.'[2]

Wainwright on the summit of Clough Head
The Eastern Fells, Clough Head p. 7

He was very clear in his view that mountains represented a challenge to fulfil and attain by dint of hard physical effort that mirrored one's resolve to be a better person in life. He summed up his feelings in his semi-autobiographical book, *Fellwanderer*, written at the conclusion of his series of the Pictorial Guides:

> 'Mountain climbing satisfies an instinct all men should feel: the urge to get to the top. It is natural for a man to look up, to strive to attain something higher and out of his immediate reach, to overcome the difficulties and disappointments of his upward progress, to exult at his ultimate success. Mountain climbing is an epitome of life, and good practice for it. You start at the bottom, the weaklings and the irresolute drop out on the way up, the determined reach the top. Life is like that.'[3]

Bowfell, from Lingmoor Fell
A Lakeland Sketchbook, No. 1

But other emotions and feelings inspired Wainwright to climb the hills. There was always in his mind the excitement of another day of exploration on the hills to be enjoyed to the full. It was what he called 'boyish enthusiasm'. In a reply to Bert Markland written in 1958, he looked forward to researching his next book, *The Southern Fells*:

> 'The following week found me on Lingmoor Fell, in Langdale, making a start on Book Four. I have spent the last four Sundays there in a fever of enthusiasm, and the sadness at forsaking the Central Fells has already passed. All my thoughts now are of the splendid hills running up to Bowfell and the Scafells, and the prospect of getting amongst them week after week makes me feel as excited as a little boy with a new toy.'[4]

In an unpublished letter to a Mr Kirby, he wrote:

> 'I am glad to learn that your interest in the fells, and your activities thereon, continue undiminished and that you are still well able to undertake major expeditions. Well, a man is as old as he feels, and there is no reason why you should not carry on for many years yet if you can maintain a boyish enthusiasm.'[5]

Wainwright maintained his enthusiasm for walking and climbing to the end of his life and when he was unable to climb, he could write about past adventures to inspire his readers – this written in *Ex-Fellwanderer* on the cusp of his 80th birthday:

> 'Old age? People are as old as they feel, and life to me has never advanced beyond springtime. I still have the interests and enthusiasms of a sixteen-year-old: simple enthusiasms, restricted mainly to climbing hills and writing about them. I have no feeling that winter is upon me.'[6]

Then there were emotions that were inspired by just being in the hills: drama, awe, sadness, and love.

Surely there can be no greater landscape in Britain for high drama than the mountains of Scotland. Wainwright certainly thought so. Whilst his heart was wedded to the romantic landscapes of the Lake District, his annual holiday to Scotland after the War gave him an appreciation of the grandeur and majesty of the Highlands. Perhaps there was nowhere more dramatic than Glen Coe. It was not just the intimidating aspect of the mountains that pressed in from each side of the glen, it was the history of a massacre that hung over the shattered peaks and weighed heavily on the mind of anyone passing through. For Wainwright, it was an emotional experience:

The Three Sisters of Glen Coe
Scottish Mountain Drawings, Volume Three,
The Western Highlands, No. 190

'Glen Coe is high drama. The scenery is tremendously impressive. It is the best known of all the Scottish glens – famous for its tragic history, an international reputation as a climbing ground where mountaineers and cragsmen can test their skills but, especially when under snow, dangerous for lesser fry and providing an emotional experience for all who come this way. The glen is a deep cutting between intimidating mountains: one side is formed by a serrated ridge difficult to attain and more difficult to traverse; on the other side are three savage and near-vertical buttresses of daunting aspect. These are known as the Three Sisters of Glen Coe, strangely because there is certainly nothing feminine about them; they are brutally masculine, threatening and, when wreathed in swirling mist, even frightening. Glen Coe is no place for the timid.'[7]

Pillar Rock and Robinson's Cairn
Lakeland Mountain Drawings, Volume One, No. 94

A few scenes in Lakeland inspired awe or even fear, places such as Mickledore, Scafell Crag, Wastwater or, as in this example, Pillar Rock as seen from Robinson's Cairn on the High Level Traverse to the summit of Pillar. Wainwright recalled his walks on this route to one of his regular correspondents, Margaret Ainley, in 1984:

'But obviously your most perfect day of all was the visit to Wasdale and the round of Mosedale. Your graphic account of this day's adventures was a classic. Every moment of it was a joy, the highlight being the sudden awesome sight of Pillar Rock from

Robinson's Cairn, and I agree with you that this is perhaps the grandest sight in the district and a memorable emotional experience, more so if you are alone. I think I mention in my new book[8] that the scenery here is so overpowering that even toothache can be forgotten,...'[9]

On many occasions, Wainwright expressed sadness or sorrow in his writing but it was usually associated with unwelcome changes in the landscape or when Nature was damaged by the actions of man. It is surprising, therefore, to find Wainwright in melancholy mood on the summit of Scafell. It is the realisation that there will come a time when he will no longer be able to climb to the high summits, but will be left only with memories:

'... Scafell's top is a most excellent viewpoint and, additionally, a place for reverie, especially when reached from the north, for here there is awareness that one has come at last to the outer edge of the mountains and that, beyond, lie only declining foothills to the sea. Vaguely, in the mind of a fellwalker long past his youth, there arises a feeling of sadness, as though at this point the mountains are behind, in the past, and ahead is a commonplace world, a future in which mountains have no part, his own future.'[10]

However, he was more sanguine in his later years when exploring the lesser heights of Lakeland in *The Outlying Fells of Lakeland*, although one detects a note of regret as he reclines in comfort on Beacon Fell thinking of younger, more carefree days when his objective would have been Great Gable:

'Beacon Fell ranks amongst the most delectable of the lesser heights of Lakeland. It is an epitome of all that appeals to fellwalkers. The approach is a joy: lovely and colourful terrain rich in trees and dense thickets of juniper relieved occasionally by marshy flats of myrtle and dry banks of bracken. Higher, grey rocks outcrop in haphazard array and heather and bilberry carpet the rough ground. The paths are enchanting, full of little surprises, while the streams are crystal clear. There is a tarn, too, hidden in a fold of the hills. But it is the summit, abrupt and rocky, and the far-reaching view that make the ascent so worth while. One can recline in comfort here and almost feel sorry for youngsters who, at this moment, are toiling up Great Gable.'[11]

Scafell Pike and Ill Crag, from Throstle Garth
A Lakeland Sketchbook, No. 2

Perhaps the strongest emotion that stirred in Wainwright's soul was his love of the hills and mountains that had become true and steadfast friends. And it was this love of the high places that he wanted to impart to his readers because he understood that turning to the hills could bring an opportunity to re-assess busy lives and, while doing so, find inner peace.

In a memorable piece of writing, he sums up these feelings perfectly in his Soliloquy inspired by climbing to the summit of Lakeland's highest fell, Scafell Pike:

> 'Why *does* a man climb mountains? Why has he forced his tired and sweating body up here when he might instead have been sitting at his ease in a deckchair at the seaside, looking at girls in bikinis, or fast asleep, or sucking ice-cream, according to his fancy. On the face of it the thing doesn't make sense.

Emotional Revelations

Yet more and more people are turning to the hills; they find something in these wild places that can be found nowhere else. It may be solace for some, satisfaction for others: the joy of exercising muscles that modern ways of living have cramped, perhaps; or a balm for jangled nerves in the solitude and silence of the peaks; or escape from the clamour and tumult of everyday existence. It may have something to do with a man's subconscious search for beauty, growing keener as so much in the world grows uglier. It may be a need to re-adjust his sights, to get out of his own narrow groove and climb above it to see wider horizons and truer perspectives. In a few cases it may even be a curiosity inspired by *A Wainwright's* Pictorial Guides. Or it may be, and for most walkers it *will* be, quite simply, a deep love of the hills, a love that has grown over the years, whatever motive first took them there: a feeling that these hills are friends, tried and trusted friends, always there when needed.

It is a question every man must answer for himself.'[12]

This simple philosophy was repeated in his replies to letters he received from his legion of readers. One such reply was to Joy Ross, a keen wild swimmer, who had used the Pictorial Guides to map every tarn and pool that was suitable for swimming:

'Thankyou very much for your interesting letter, and its kind (too kind) references to myself. Reading it made me blush, but I am, of course, very pleased to learn that my books are proving helpful. . . .

You will love Lakeland more and more with growing familiarity – the sincerest test of affection – and you will find it equally charming at all seasons. I hope you continue to enjoy your expeditions to the hills, for no experiences are more rewarding. Every day on the tops is different from all others, whether you seek beauty, excitement, lovely views or merely exercise; every day has its individual memories. Even the soakings and weariness and bad moments are pleasant in retrospect!'[13]

It was these sweet memories that Wainwright treasured and stored in his heart to recall with pleasure in quiet moments, or at troubled times in his life. In his introduction to *The Eastern Fells*, he wrote of Lakeland: 'its enchantment grows with passing years and quiet eventide is enriched by the haunting sweetness of dear memories, memories that remain evergreen through the flight of time, that refresh and sustain in the darker days.'[14]

And what a store of memories he had, recalling many at the end of the Pictorial Guide series in *Fellwanderer*:

Dalegarth Force
A Fifth Lakeland Sketchbook, No. 371
'the more intimate charm of sparkling waterfalls in ferny dells'

'Not so much the scenes preferred by the tourists—Ashness Bridge, Friar's Crag, Orrest Head—charming though they are, but the unexpected scenes, those revealed by a movement of mist, those that dramatically come into view on the last few steps to a summit cairn, those that stop a walker in his tracks as he rounds a corner and glimpses a picture beautiful beyond belief, those that occur in early morning when the sun breaks through the mist over the valley, or in the evening when one is loth to leave the peace of the tops and enjoys the reward of perfect sunsets. Or the memories in miniature, the more intimate charm of sparkling waterfalls in ferny dells, of winter birches touched by sunlight against a dark sky, of squirrels running along a wall, of trees laden with new snow, of translucent waters in rocky pools, of lonely rowans splashing grey rocks with vivid colour, of hovering buzzards motionless in the sky and ravens in tumbling flight, of wood-smoke rising lazily from farm chimneys in the quiet of evening, of sheepdogs watching intently every movement of their masters and refusing to be distracted, of newborn lambs and their proud mothers. Oh, a pen cannot tell of these joys. A walk in Lakeland is a walk in heaven.'[15]

So, for Wainwright, a walk in Lakeland was a walk in heaven. But he realised that although he could describe his memories he was quite unable to convey the feelings and emotions he experienced from just being in this magical landscape. The reason was very simple; emotions could only be felt, not expressed in words:

'My space is nearly finished. I could have used it better, but the words that would more adequately tell the glory of the fells are not known to me. Like a lover who can only keep repeating the same three words because there are no others that say more, I have found the pen, in my hands, no instrument for describing the captivating charm of Lakeland. Lakeland is an emotion, and emotions are felt, not expressed.'[16]

On his first visit to Lakeland with his cousin in 1930, they arrived at Keswick on the evening of the third day after a very wet crossing of Striding Edge in sluicing rain. Their hostess at a B&B in Stanger Street lent them clothes to wear and the next day they explored the surrounding area finding a pleasant spot to rest above the hamlet of Millbeck where there was a glorious view of the Newlands valley with its surround of delectable mountains. Nearly six decades later, Wainwright wrote in his autobiography: 'It was a scene of perfection, of flawless beauty, and I saw it through eyes dim with tears: it was an emotional revelation of splendour far beyond my imaginings.'[17]

That phrase, 'an emotional revelation of splendour far beyond my imaginings', underlines the importance Wainwright attached to imagination. The scene before his eyes went beyond what he had anticipated and he was moved to tears. Envisioning the landscape through its history and traditions, together with the ruined buildings and structures that each told a story of its past, was the key for a fuller appreciation of the varied terrain of upland Britain. Wainwright possessed an inquiring mind and a lively imagination that brought the landscape to life for his readers. It was a recognition of man's influence in shaping the natural world over millennia of occupation.

NOTES

[1] *Collected Letters of Samuel Taylor Coleridge, Vol II*, edited by Earl Leslie Griggs, p. 916

[2] *The Eastern Fells*, Some Personal Notes in conclusion

[3] *Fellwanderer*, unpaginated

[4] *The Wainwright Letters*, edited by Hunter Davies, p. 104

[5] *Letter to Mr Kirby*, 14th April 1966 (unpublished)

[6] *Ex-Fellwanderer*, unpaginated

[7] *Wainwright in Scotland*, p. 134

[8] The new book was *Fellwalking with Wainwright*. Worldly worries are totally excluded from the mind, and even toothache can be forgotten in such sensational surroundings.' p. 200

[9] *Letter to Margaret Ainley*, 15th August 1984 (unpublished)

[10] *The Southern Fells*, Scafell p. 15

[11] *The Outlying Fells of Lakeland*, p. 98

[12] *The Southern Fells*, Scafell Pike p. 24

[13] *The Wainwright Letters*, edited by Hunter Davies, p. 118

[14] *The Eastern Fells*, Introduction

[15] *Fellwanderer*, unpaginated

[16] *Fellwanderer*, unpaginated

[17] *Ex-Fellwanderer*, unpaginated

CHAPTER SEVEN

Imagining the Past

The Romantic poets believed that imagination was a creative power of the human mind. Coleridge explored the philosophy of poetic imagination in his writing and lectures. He believed that the power of imagination allowed a poet to think and feel like another being. But in the mind, this power had to be one of sensibility and subtlety enabling the poet to perceive that which could not be heard, seen or felt in the everyday world.

In a letter to William Sotheby, written in 1802, Coleridge explained his theory using three images that described the process of poetic imagination at work:

> '... for all sounds & forms of human nature, he must have the *ear* of a wild Arab listening in the silent Desert, the *eye* of a North American Indian tracing the footsteps of an Enemy upon the Leaves that strew the Forest—; the *Touch* of a Blind Man feeling the face of a darling Child— ...'[1]

* * * * * * *

Wainwright did not propound theories of imagination in his writing, but he emphasised its importance in enabling a person to use the power of the imagination to perceive, in the mind's eye, past human behaviour and events that helped shape the landscape that we see today.

Wainwright acquired much of his knowledge of the story of the landscape from a study of maps, always his favourite reading material. His fascination with maps began as a small child when he was given a map of Lancashire and he spent many hours studying the map, using it to plan his explorations of the countryside that encompassed Blackburn. His eye was drawn to the areas coloured brown that denoted the surrounding hills and his curiosity was aroused, wondering what he would find there. He described these early wanderings in his autobiography:

A Newt in Hard Tarn

'I was different too in my liking for long solitary walks. Someone had given me a map of Lancashire, a tattered sheet on a small scale but it opened a bit more of the world for me, and I was eager to learn. For the first time I could see the surrounding towns and villages of which I had heard in relation to Blackburn, and the roads linking them. I treasured that old map and studied it intently, planning walks to places new to me. In due course I walked all the roads and visited all the urban communities within reach, but I was especially attracted to the land coloured brown on the map indicating land over 1000 feet: in these areas there were no roads and few habitations; they were wildernesses in my youthful imagination, places to explore. . . . I often tramped twenty miles in a day's walk, interested in all I saw; I liked looking around corners at fresh scenes. These early excursions out of sight and sound of the towns bred in me a love of lonely uplands that has persisted ever since, and a fascination for maps that has never faded; . . .'[2]

Until the end of the War, the only maps available were 1-inch maps produced by the Ordnance Survey and Bartholomew's. There was very little historical detail on these maps. On his first visit to Lakeland in 1930, he was intrigued by the reference to a Roman Road and it was his first expedition to walk along the route over the High Street range from Windermere to Pooley Bridge.

In the late 1940s, Ordnance Survey began to publish the series of 2½-inch maps that gave much greater detail about man-made landscape features. Wainwright used these maps to produce his own in the Pictorial Guides. He also had access to an old set of 6-inch maps that gave him further details of the industrial history of Lakeland.

When he was out on the fells, he was using all these sources of information to look for, and find, these features on the ground and he was able to build a picture of the different layers of history in the Lake District landscape. He used his vivid imagination to fill in the gaps and visualise the lives of the people who inhabited this landscape in ages past.

One such place was the summit of High Street in the far eastern fells. High Street is an exhilarating climb but the top is gently domed and featureless save for a broken drystone wall and a trigonometrical station. But armed with the knowledge he had gleaned from his study of maps, Wainwright brought the summit to life.

Imagining the Past

As he wrote in *The Far Eastern Fells*:

> 'The summit is barren of scenic interest, and only visitors of lively imagination will fully appreciate their surroundings. Any person so favoured may recline on the turf and witness, in his mind's eye, a varied pageant of history...'[3]

The summit of High Street
The Far Eastern Fells, High Street, p. 10

In a later book, he imagined the lives of the people who had worked and played on that remote summit over the past 2000 years:

> 'One needs to be alone and blessed with imagination to fully appreciate High Street. Then in the mind's eye one can see the weary and dispirited legions of Roman soldiers on their long march, far from homes and families, strangers in a hostile land, thinking of themselves not as conquerors but as exiles from the sunny villages they had left behind. Or one can imagine the lively carousels of the dalesfolk at their annual meetings here in past centuries, the feastings, the wrestling, the horse racing and other sports, all combining to make the event their greatest day of the year. Or one can think of the men who built the stone wall two hundred years ago, finding their own material and sleeping on the

site for pay of eightpence a day. Today, all these are forgotten men and only the mountain survives, now in perfect peace.'[4]

Wainwright had a vivid imagination that needed no map to transport himself back in time. On his Pennine Journey walk in 1938, his route northwards to the Roman Wall took him to Blanchland at the end of a long tramp of twenty-six miles over rough moorland roads that were hard on the feet, but entering Blanchland through a stone arch as the light was fading was like stepping back into a medieval scene from history.

In his fevered imagination, Wainwright pictured a scene from the Middle Ages, not walking through the entrance with a rucksack on his back and a stick in his hand, but an armoured knight on horseback carrying a lance ready for anything: rescuing a maid in distress, jousting on the green, or more incongruously, demonstrating his prowess as a bullfighter:

> 'When you set foot in Blanchland, you step into the Middle Ages; it is its strange, medieval appearance you remember it by. You feel oddly out of place as you wander through the old stone arch and enter the square courtyard which is the heart of the village. It is fantastic that you should walk into this old-world military camp with a rucksack on your back; you should gallop in on a fiery steed, bending low to avoid the arch, and pull up with a flourish amid a cloud of dust. A sports coat and flannels make you grotesque here; clanking armour is the men's wear. Your walking-stick should be a glittering lance.
>
> Your imagination is indeed impoverished if you can enter this picturesque village for the first time and not thrill at the spectacle it affords. Especially if you see it in the gloaming, as I saw it, in the magic moment when it is neither day nor night. For then, you cannot be quite sure that you are not dreaming, that your eyes are not bewitched. I responded magnificently. I was centuries back in history. My thoughts were a jumble of the Holy Grail and the Round Table, of St George and the Dragon, of Galahad and Lancelot and Horatio on the bridge. And Blanchland, after all, is not as old as these.
>
> My eye flashed as I looked round the dim square. Now, damsel in distress, scream! Now, hand me my lance and lead me to the joust! Now, matador, loose the bull! I was ready for anything.'[5]

Imagining the Past

The following morning in the cold light of day, the spell was broken and he had returned to twentieth-century reality:

'Blanchland in the morning is a different place from Blanchland in the evening. It still appeals to the imagination, most vividly, but it has not the magic power to transport you back through the ages. Blanchland in the morning is twentieth century; there are the walls and towers and architecture of the past, but I was conscious as I looked at them that these were created long ago, before my time; not, as I felt last night, that they were contemporary. Other things there are, too, which heighten the contrast and destroy the illusion: petrol pumps, road signs, a modern post office. Still, Blanchland is unique and its setting is lovely. It is a place for a honeymoon.'[6]

On any walk, one might come across the remains of an abandoned industrial site, such as a disused railway trackbed, which, for Wainwright, provided the stimulus to revive memories of playing 'trains' as a child. On his long-distance Coast to Coast walk, the disused track of the Rosedale Ironstone Railway, faithfully following the contours around the head of Farndale, was the inspiration for an imaginative return to childhood:

Bloworth Crossing
A Coast to Coast Walk, p. 141

'At Bloworth Crossing, the walking becomes dead easy as the railway track is followed for six miles around many sinuous curves and on the same contour all the way. The rails have been taken up and the permanent way has grown grass, but it offers a journey of pure delight to walkers with youthful minds who can imagine themselves speeding along in charge of a locomotive.'[7]

The long embankment near Esklets

The disused trackbed of the Rosedale Ironstone Railway, Farndale
A Coast to Coast Walk, p. 143

'Fast walking continues along the railway track and speeds will now have accelerated to 5 m.p.h. . . .

Youth hostellers bound for Westerdale should also turn off here, rejoining our route next morning at Rosedale Head.

The rest of us will resist the attractions of lovely Farndale (which specialises in daffodils, not beds) and surge on happily along the permanent way. We're enjoying this: it's like playing at trains again. Better than that, it's like being a train yourself.'[8]

It was not only man-made features that aroused his interest. In his early explorations of the Lake District he was eager to visit two peaks whose names alone had the power to capture his imagination: Pillar and Steeple in the western fells. But their remote location put them out of bounds for many years and even when he moved to Kendal in 1941, wartime travel restrictions constrained his ambitions. When the opportunity came to climb to their summits he was disappointed. Their alluring names did not live up to the reality; Pillar was a grassy, flat-topped summit and Steeple was not as sharply pointed as its name suggested. He recalled the story in *Wainwright's Favourite Lakeland Mountains*:

'When I was a young man my visits to the Lake District were of necessity restricted to day excursions on the train to Windermere and, in due course, I became very familiar with the glorious countryside within a ten-mile radius of the railway station. I longed to be able to get further afield. Studying the Ordnance Survey map of the district was a daily ritual for me

Imagining the Past

over many years: I knew the details by heart although most of the region remained out of reach. I pinpointed all the mountains on the map, these having an exciting attraction for me: we had valleys and hills at home but no mountains. In particular, two mountain names fired my imagination: in the western fells were Pillar and Steeple, and for twenty years they plagued my mind until I was able to see and set foot on them. Even when I moved to Kendal, thereby bringing all the mountains within closer range, wartime restrictions on travel kept me in exile. At last the chance came for a visit to Wasdale Head and I set forth eagerly to realise a long ambition and see the promised pinnacles.

They were disappointing. Pillar was nothing like a pillar and Steeple bore only a slight resemblance to a steeple.'[9]

Pillar
The Western Fells, Pillar, p. 1

However, as Wainwright was to discover, the glory of Pillar was Pillar Rock, first named by shepherds and known as The Pillar. As he wrote in his chapter on the fell: 'Men of letters could not have chosen better.'[10]

And as he came to know the area more intimately, Steeple did not disappoint. Steeple features in the list of his six favourite summits, all having the attributes of: 'a small neat peak of naked rock with a good view'.[11]

In his chapter about the fell, he acknowledged that the name was an inspiration and well-chosen:

> 'The unknown man who first named this fell was blessed both with inspiration and imagination. Few mountains given descriptive names have fared better. *Steeple* is a magnificent choice. Seen on a map, it commands the eye and quickens the pulse; seen in reality, it does the same. The climbing of Steeple is a feat to announce with pride in a letter to the old folks at home, who can safely be relied upon to invest the writer with undeserved heroism. Fancy our Fred having climbed a steeple!'[12]

Steeple
The Western Fells, Steeple, p. 3

Imagining the Past

Seen from Scoat Fell, as in his sketch, the summit looked unassailable, but Wainwright revealed that its top could be attained by a simple ridge walk where one could sit alone, in silence and contemplate the magnificent view:

'From the summit ridge of Scoat Fell, Steeple is seen in profile, its east face overlooking Windgap Cove being manifestly impossible, but its neat summit, where one can sit like a king on his throne, can in fact be gained by a mere stroll from the ridge on a clear path. And should be. To be alone on Steeple's tiny top with no other person in sight, is an emotive experience long remembered.'[13]

Imagination could stir the emotions, inducing feelings of unease or fear of unseen hazards. Wainwright thought this could happen to timid walkers at the sight of Gordale Scar in the Dales:

'Gordale Scar is a towering amphitheatre of naked limestone, and its vertical walls come into sight suddenly, and with a shattering effect on the senses, as a rocky corner is turned on the approach. Boulders scattered around, obviously fallen from the impending crags, give the imaginative visitor a feeling of unease. Adventurous mortals may climb up by the waterfall to a higher gorge, but most are content to halt at the portals, overawed by the hostile scene and doubtful of their welcome.'[14]

Gordale Scar
A Dales Sketchbook, No. 64

Wainwright could bring the past to life through the power of his imagination. Everywhere he travelled, he would try to imagine the past in sympathy with the harsh realities of life of the people who lived there.

The old road over Shap Fells, on the incline above Hause Foot
Old Roads of Eastern Lakeland, p. 66

In his book, *Old Roads of Eastern Lakeland*, he traced the routes of old droveways and packhorse trails and in places found the original paths, now long abandoned by the modern road network. He was able to empathise with the itinerant workers who trod these long-forgotten ways:

'Walkers who are blessed with imaginative minds and a knowledge of history will especially enjoy travelling these ancient ways. They will tread in the steps of men long forgotten: traders, cattle drovers, miners, tinkers and pedlars who journeyed on foot over rough ground in all weathers, not for pleasure for there was little pleasure in travel in those far off days; and will appreciate the sufferings of these early pioneers as they toiled across uncharted and shelterless fells.
They were the first fellwalkers.'[15]

Imagining the Past

Writing about Hardknott Castle in *The Southern Fells*, he was concerned that reconstruction and preservation of the remaining fabric of the site would reduce its imaginative appeal. He asked:

> '. . . would not the mouldering ruins, left to their natural decay, have had a greater appeal to the imagination?'[16]

His reflections dwelt on the soldiers that lived in this remote spot in a land far from the warmer climes of home:

> 'One wonders what were the thoughts of the sentries as they kept watch over this lonely outpost amongst the mountains, nearly two thousand years ago? Did they admire the massive architecture of the Scafell group as they looked north, the curve of the valley from source to sea as their eyes turned west? Or did they feel themselves to be unwanted strangers in a harsh and hostile land? Did their hearts ache for the sunshine of their native country, for their families, for their homes?'[17]

The north gate, Hardknott Roman Fort
A Second Lakeland Sketchbook, No. 106

A Newt in Hard Tarn

During his explorations of the Lake District for his Pictorial Guides, Wainwright would seek out long-abandoned industrial sites that had been indicated on large-scale maps of the district. There was a network of forgotten pathways that often led high into the mountains where he located the remains of mine workings and quarries. His thoughts were for the people who laboured in these derelict, forsaken places, people who had hopes and dreams that were shattered when their workplaces finally closed:

The copper mine at the foot of Gable Crag, Dale Head
A Second Lakeland Sketchbook, No. 108

'Copper mining was a major industry, while on the Honister flank huge slices were gouged out of the fellside by slate quarries;

both enterprises are long abandoned, being fatal casualties in the march of progress. Today Dale Head is an industrial graveyard, a mouldering museum of relics of former activity, a place haunted by the ghosts of men who once laboured here. I am always saddened when I see ruins, especially those in lonely places where conditions must have been primitive. I find myself trying to imagine the folk who lived and worked there in happier days with no thought of the fate that was to befall them, of the heartbreak of their final departure, taking their memories and leaving behind so much to rot and decay. Ruins are the burial grounds of hopes and aspirations.'[18]

There was sadness in his heart when he thought of the despair and anguish caused by the closure of the mines and quarries, but he was determined that generations of labourers should not be consigned to history and forgotten. He could honour their memory by preserving the heritage of their achievements in his books. By diligent study of the old maps, he sought out the remains of these industrial sites and recorded their passing in finely-drawn pen and ink sketches and illuminating descriptions. It was his legacy to a past way of life.

NOTES

[1] *Collected Letters of Samuel Taylor Coleridge, Vol II*, edited by Earl Leslie Griggs, p. 810

[2] *Ex-Fellwanderer*, unpaginated

[3] *The Far Eastern Fells*, High Street p. 10

[4] *Wainwright's Favourite Lakeland Mountains*, p. 137

[5] *A Pennine Journey*, pp. 69-70

[6] *A Pennine Journey*, pp. 75-6

[7] *Wainwright's Coast to Coast Walk*, p. 171

[8] *A Coast to Coast Walk*, p. 143

[9] *Wainwright's Favourite Lakeland Mountains*, p. 163

[10] *The Western Fells*, Pillar p. 2

[11] *The Western Fells*, Some Personal Notes in conclusion

[12] *The Western Fells*, Steeple p. 2

[13] *Fellwalking with a Camera*, unpaginated

[14] *A Dales Sketchbook*, No. 64

[15] *Old Roads of Eastern Lakeland*, Introduction, p. vii

[16] *The Southern Fells*, Hard Knott p. 2

17 *The Southern Fells*, Hard Knott p. 2
18 *Wainwright's Favourite Lakeland Mountains*, p. 51

CHAPTER EIGHT

Industrial Landscapes

B ritish Romanticism developed at a time of significant social change brought about by the quickening pace of the Industrial Revolution during the eighteenth century. The Romantic poets were concerned about the damaging effects of industrialisation: the threat to Nature as the countryside became home to the new textile mills and the workers that were housed there and the negative effects on family life were part of the philosophical discussion in poems such as *The Excursion* (*see* pp. 22-3).

Wainwright's response to the effects of industrialisation and mechanisation and the decline of craft skills on upland landscapes and the countryside, together with the social and environmental changes this brought to British society during the twentieth century, will form the themes of the final chapters of this book.

* * * * * * *

By the time that Wainwright began to explore the hills and mountains of northern England, the heyday of industrial mining enterprise in the Pennines and the Lake District was past, a victim of cheaper foreign imports of raw materials such as copper and lead. Uneconomic mines were forced to close and the workforce had no choice but to seek employment in the cities, or, for some, emigration was the answer. Communities perished, leaving the decaying remains of the industrial infrastructure and dwellings of the former employees. In these abandoned settlements dreams had withered and hope had died. Wainwright articulated his feelings in his book, *A Pennine Journey,* when he passed through Rookhope, a former mining village, on his way from Weardale to Blanchland in the Derwent valley. What he saw affected him deeply. He felt that Rookhope was a metaphor of his own personal troubles, one of the reasons why he had escaped from the situation at home into the peace and tranquillity of the northern Pennines. But here he was reminded most forcibly of his own shattered hopes and dreams:

'Once it must have been a place of considerable activity, for there were lead mines and smelting mills and a mineral railway threaded the winding valley. But the days of prosperity are gone from Rookhope, and only the hideous scars remain. No desolation is so complete as the desolation of abandoned dwellings, and here they are in plenty, crumbling ruins where once was bustling activity, death where there was life. I never see a ruin without wondering what the man who planned the building, and stood back and admired his finished work, would think now of his proud creation, what sadness would fill his breast. Tragedies such as this are all around us, in our own lives. We have all built our dream-castles and seen them crumble to dust, sadly if the neglect has been our own, bitterly if someone we loved and trusted has failed us.'[1]

A decade later, he was living in Kendal and planning his own 'love letter'[2] to Lakeland. By diligent study of his maps, he discovered that there were many old industrial sites scattered throughout the district, often in remote mountain fastnesses, difficult of access and it was his particular joy to seek out these hidden places far off the beaten track. It was Lakeland's forgotten history:

'. . . I have preferred most the secret places that must be searched for, the drove roads and neglected packhorse trails, the ruins of abandoned industries, the adits and levels and shafts of the old mines and quarries, the wild gullies and ravines that rarely see a two-legged visitor. The beauty of the Lake District is there for all to see. The glory of the mountains is there for all to see who climb. The secrets are for those who wander from the trodden ways.'[3]

'The 2½-inch maps quickened my interest in the detail of the fells, and it was a thirst for this knowledge that led me in due course to use the Ordnance maps on a scale of 6 inches to the mile, which provided still greater detail, such as sheepfolds, boundary posts and mine levels. And, because the 6-inch maps had not been completely revised for a great many years, and were thus in this respect out of date, they presented a fascinating picture of Lakeland as it was around the turn of the century and

Industrial Landscapes

indicated the roads and paths engineered to serve the mines and quarries and sheepfolds since abandoned. It became a joy to me to trace these old ways by which now-forgotten men had journeyed to and from now-forgotten places of employment. The 6-inch maps quickened my interest, and stimulated my imagination, in industrial Lakeland.'[4]

Catbells and Newlands
A Lakeland Sketchbook, No. 37

It might seem surprising that for someone who wrote so much about the romantic charm and beauty of Lakeland, the industrial history of the district could provoke such interest and fascination. However, Wainwright came to realise that prior to the growing tourist interest of the nineteenth century, one of the main sources of employment in the Lake District was mining and quarrying. Despite some unsightly scars left after the mines and quarries closed, he came to regard this as an important part of the shaping of the Lakeland landscape. When he first saw the valley of Newlands, he was moved to tears by the beauty of the scene. But there was the debris of former industries, which, for Wainwright, was all part of Lakeland's heritage:

> 'The beauty of the valley is not without blemishes. For centuries, in addition to the agricultural interests introduced by the early settlers, men have torn holes in the fellsides to extract the stone needed for their buildings, and have burrowed deep into the ground in search of the more valuable subterranean treasures of lead and copper and even the most precious, gold. These mining activities have long ceased and the workings abandoned for Nature to heal. For the present, these places of honest endeavour remain to be seen, some of them traps for unwary walkers, but I prefer to regard them not as ugly scars but as site museums that form an integral part of Lakeland's history. Newlands is not ashamed of its pockmarks but proud of them.'[5]

Scenes of industrial history became an important part of Wainwright's books, recorded for posterity in his sketches and descriptions:

Loughrigg Cave
A Third Lakeland Sketchbook, No. 211

Industrial Landscapes

'Quarrying is a major industry in Lakeland, the local stone being much in evidence in the buildings and walls of the district and having gained an international reputation for its colour and texture and durability. Unlike coarser stone, won by surface excavation, many of Lakeland's quarries are worked underground. Loughrigg Cave is a manmade cavern of imposing proportions. The workers have gone from it and left a colourful fairy grotto.'[6]

The importance of his work can be demonstrated in this example, a disused spinning mill in the Wyre valley that Wainwright photographed shortly before it was demolished, two centuries after it was built:

The old mill at Dolphinholme
A Wyre Sketchbook, No. 15

'The mill at Lower Dolphinholme was built in 1784 for the spinning of worsted, its machinery being driven by water diverted from the nearby Wyre, but fell into decline and was closed in 1869. The mill served the community well, providing employment and housing, a gas supply for the village and even a chapel; after closure it was used as a village hall until falling into ruin. The mill race can still be seen but the building was demolished recently, a big part of Dolphinholme's history going with it.'[7]

A Newt in Hard Tarn

Whilst the demise of upland industries had the social consequences of unemployment and depopulation in places such as Rookhope, there were unwelcome effects on the landscape in other areas.

In *Fellwalking with Wainwright*, he offered the opinion that: 'No mountain in Lakeland has been more cruelly exploited than Coniston Old Man.'[8] Despite the devastation in the Coppermines Valley, Wainwright advised his readers to lift their eyes above valley level to the surrounding summits, a sight that would gladden the heart:

Coppermines Valley, Coniston
A Fourth Lakeland Sketchbook, No. 265

'This hollow among the hills presents a surprising scene of squalid desolation, typical of the dreary outskirts of many coalmining towns but utterly foreign to the Lake District, and it says much for the quality of the encircling mountains that they can triumph over the serious disfigurement of ugly spoil heaps and gaping wounds, and still look majestic. Here, in this strange amphitheatre, where flowers once grew, one sees the hopeless debris of the ruins of industries long abandoned, where flowers will never grow again, and, as always in the presence of death, is saddened – but a raising of the eyes discloses a surround of noble heights, and then the heart is uplifted too.'[9]

At the southern end of Windermere, the closure of the bobbin mill brought sadness at the loss of the old machines and the skilled craftsmen that manufactured bobbins from locally-produced wood, now discarded in favour of factory-made plastic:

'With the closure of the bobbin works at Stott Park, Finsthwaite, in 1971 another of Lakeland's rural industries came to a sad end. Formerly there were scores of such works, many with their own coppice woods, serving the cotton industry, but the coming of cheap plastics has driven wood bobbins from favour and the ingenious machines used in manufacture are fated to be dead museum pieces.'[10]

Bobbin works, Stott Park
A Fourth Lakeland Sketchbook, No. 295

A Newt in Hard Tarn

When he was researching the route of the Pennine Way, Wainwright was shocked when he dropped down from the high Pennine moors into the valley of the River Calder, describing the scene as one where: 'the eye recoils from the industrial blight immediately in front – a stagnant canal, a dirty river, a busy road and a railway crowded side by side.'[11]

In a later book he described it as an area of crowded industrial development within the narrow confines of a steep-sided valley and only in a few places was it possible for the eye of the imagination to discern former scenes of beauty:

The Calder Valley
A Second Dales Sketchbook, No. 147

'Road, railway, river and canal jostle for space along the narrow floor of the Calder Valley between Todmorden and Hebden Bridge, and mills and cottages add to the congestion, there being little left to please the eye. Before industry took over, however, the valley was green and threaded only by a clear river and a country lane, and the view of it from the high ground adjoining must have been quite lovely. It is still possible, from vantage points on either side, to imagine the rural scene that has since been destroyed.'[12]

Industrial Landscapes

However, Wainwright realised that Nature was a great healer and, over time, long-abandoned industrial sites could be softened by natural regeneration, although it was rare for all traces of former industrial activity to be erased. The scene below is encountered on the route of *A Coast to Coast Walk* whilst traversing the escarpment of the Cleveland Hills:

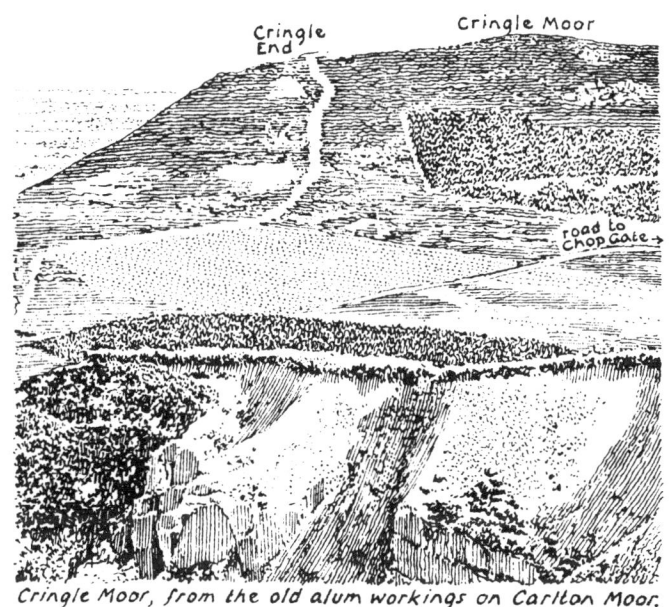

Cringle Moor, from the old alum workings on Carlton Moor
A Coast to Coast Walk, p. 130

'The broad expanse of moorland extending for 30 miles from the Vale of Mowbray to the east coast, heatherclad, unenclosed, uninhabited, remote from industry and noise and free from traffic, is a magnificent territory for the walker: open country like the Pennines and the Cheviots yet more handsome and colourful – and friendlier by far. . . . Today it is hard to believe that these uplands were formerly exploited for the wealth below the surface, but in fact they have been worked extensively for iron and coal, and, distinctively, for jet and alum. These industries are now all abandoned and nature is hiding their traces although the tracks of the mineral railways, the iron workings and jet spoilheaps are likely to be permanent reminders.'[13]

Wainwright was passionate that the industrial past should not be simply forgotten, that the ruins of the old mines be left to crumble and decay. He was convinced that future generations could learn from the past; not only about the processes of extraction, but also about the people who laboured in the mines – their skills that were in danger of being lost, their lives and their fortitude in the face of poverty.

The route of *A Coast to Coast Walk* traverses the lead mining area in Swaledale, where there are many examples of the former mines with their processing sheds. In his guidebook, Wainwright made an impassioned plea that at least one of the mine complexes should be preserved as a museum:

Old Gang Smelt Mill, Swaledale
A Coast to Coast Walk, p. 92

'In the triangle of land between Swaledale and Arkengarthdale particularly the scene even today is one of sterile devastation, despoliation, decay ... There is no beauty in these sorry ruins but a great fascination for those of imagination who can picture in their minds the scene as it was a century before and still more for those who have the knowledge to piece together the fragments that remain.

There is a great need, before everything crumbles to dust, to preserve at least one of the mines as a site museum, not necessarily restoring the smelt and crushing mills and opening up the levels but reclaiming enough to demonstrate the methods of operation and the tools and equipment used, with a plan of the workings, graphs of annual output, and such supporting documentary records as may still be available. This could perhaps be done by one of the Universities or archaeological groups, and should be financed from Government funds.

Our route takes us through the heart of the lead mining district yet gives only a faint insight of the vast area explored and exploited for ore. But note especially the Blakethwaite and Old Gang workings, which we pass, either one of which could be adapted for 20th century study and, it might well be hoped, for 20th century appreciation of the initiative, industry and ingenuity of men who lived hard, in times less favoured than those of today.

We have lost too much of the past through concern for the present.'[14]

It was the experiences of the workers that Wainwright wanted to preserve. This would be their legacy and acknowledge their contribution to the industrial history of this country. Wainwright took immense pride in the achievements of the Victorian railway engineers and the workforce of navvies who built the infrastructure, much of which has survived intact. One of the great edifices to survive was the Ribblehead Viaduct, the location of which, in difficult terrain, presented a complex engineering problem. But in his commentary, it was the labourers that he honoured:

'Alongside [the viaduct] was the 'shanty town' of the workers, who suffered great privations and many deaths. The viaduct is their monument.'[15]

In a later book, he retold the story of the building of the viaduct, a story of hardship for both the men and their families who lived out on the moor in desperate conditions, many not surviving the harsh environment or the accidents that occurred during construction:

'East of the Ribblehead railway viaduct and almost in its evening shadow is the desolate moorland of Batty Green[16], an inhospitable tract of rough ground without distinguishing landmarks and apparently devoid of interest except to grazing sheep, with nothing to earn a second glance by motorists on the Ingleton—Hawes road alongside. A thousand feet above sea level and defenceless against extremes of weather, it is a wilderness where nobody would choose to live.

Yet in the 1870s, Batty Green was the centre of animated activity. Here was a shanty town of huts housing the hundreds of men engaged in the construction of the viaduct, living in discomfort with their wives and children, exposed to the elements and suffering a toll of casualties resulting from hardship and adverse conditions. These rough men did a magnificent job, creating a work of art with primitive tools and equipment – but at a heavy price in human lives. The work finished, the dead buried and the site cleared, Batty Green reverted to a sullen silence broken now only by the occasional passage of trains, the rhythmic pulse of their wheels seeming to sound a requiem for those who perished.'[17]

Ribblehead Viaduct
A Ribble Sketchbook, No. 4

Industrial Landscapes

When Wainwright was preparing *The Western Fells* for publication in 1966, Honister Slate Mine was still a working quarry. However, by 1988, when he visited the site for his Coast to Coast television series, the mine had closed. In his reflections, he reiterated his view that these industrial sites were part of the Lakeland scene and should not be regarded as eyesores in an otherwise beautiful landscape. His thoughts were for a generation of workers who no longer had employment. For him, it was the end of an era:

Honister Crag
A Third Lakeland Sketchbook, No. 237

'It seems strange to see Honister Quarry so quiet and deserted after centuries of work have been spent on there. I think many regular visitors to the Lake District would be surprised to find it closed because they'd been used to seeing men working up there

A Newt in Hard Tarn

like little ants. They were working quite near the top of the crag where it's nearly vertical.

It is a scar on the landscape but it's such an integral part of Lakeland life that nobody really objects, and I certainly don't.

It's a honeycomb of tracks and passages and there are holes in the crag where they cut the slate. They cut great slices from it and it was brought down originally by horses and sleds. And then for a time they had a tramway which is gone completely now, right up the side there, and later, after the roads had been improved, lorries could get up there. They widened the roads, but it was a rather desperate venture because those roads are very steep.

Slate was brought down in great masses of slate, huge pieces. It was taken into the cutting sheds and cut to shape. It produced a very durable slate – good texture, attractive colour that was in great demand. Most of the cottages in the Lake District are roofed with this kind of slate.

I think Honister Quarry is a sad place now. After all the activity that's been spent here. Men laboured all their lives on this crag. And now it's just like a graveyard.'[18]

Wainwright admired the labourers from previous generations, for their hard work and ingenuity in construction often using the most primitive of tools: picks, shovels and wheelbarrows. He admired the skills of the masons whose buildings had stood the test of time. It was not just the quality of their workmanship that he held in high esteem, it was their pride in a job well done.

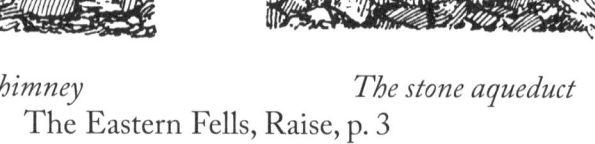

The derelict chimney   *The stone aqueduct*
The Eastern Fells, Raise, p. 3

Industrial Landscapes

While researching *The Eastern Fells* he encountered the ruins of two structures on the eastern flanks of Raise: a chimney in a state of disrepair and the remains of a stone aqueduct, each being part of the infrastructure of the Glenridding lead mine. Despite their dilapidated state, the quality of the stonework was such that Wainwright discerned both had been built by craftsmen:

> 'The lower eastern slopes of Raise are pock-marked with the scars of industry. The illustrations ... show the now-disused and derelict chimney and stone aqueduct which formerly served the Glenridding lead mine. Only a small portion of the aqueduct remains intact ... but it is sufficient to indicate the skill of the masons who built it and to make one envy their pride in the job, and be glad they are not here to see the ruins.'[19]

Wainwright was able to appreciate the quality of workmanship in the industrial ruins he found on the hills and mountains because he was a craftsman himself, a man who took immense pride in his work. The tools of his trade were a pen and ink but he shared the same sense of fulfilment as those uneducated labourers whose work revealed rare expertise and ingenuity.

However, he came to believe that the sense of pride he felt in his own work was a rarity; that the age of manufacturing on a production line was leading to slipshod attitudes in life. It was a trait he could not accept in himself and, by example, discouraged in others. He came to the conclusion that true craftsmen were rooted in history, that the world had changed and their like would not be seen again.

NOTES

[1] *A Pennine Journey*, pp. 65-6

[2] *The Eastern Fells*, Introduction

[3] *Fellwanderer*, unpaginated

[4] *Fellwanderer*, unpaginated

[5] *Wainwright in the Valleys of Lakeland*, p. 207

[6] *A Third Lakeland Sketchbook*, No. 211

[7] *A Wyre Sketchbook*, No. 15

[8] *Fellwalking with Wainwright*, p. 126

[9] *The Southern Fells*, Coniston Old Man p. 11

[10] *A Fourth Lakeland Sketchbook*, No. 295

[11] *Pennine Way Companion*, p. 139

[12] *A Second Dales Sketchbook*, No. 147

[13] *A Coast to Coast Walk*, p. 123

[14] *A Coast to Coast Walk*, pp. 86-7

[15] *A Ribble Sketchbook*, No. 4

[16] Batty Green Grid Reference: SD 764794

[17] *Wainwright in the Limestone Dales*, p. 120

[18] *Wainwright's Coast to Coast Walk*, BBC Worldwide Ltd., 2003, Programme 1, St. Bees Head to Haweswater (First screened in 1989)

[19] *The Eastern Fells*, Raise p. 3

CHAPTER NINE

True Craftsmen

Wainwright was born in the sunset years of Edwardian Britain and before the horrors of World War One brought about fundamental changes in society that accelerated throughout the twentieth century. Looking back at the end of a long life, Wainwright reflected that despite improvements in living standards many of these changes had not been for the better. Over the decades, he observed that standards had slipped, that people had less pride in their work. For Wainwright, the days of the craftsmen were largely over, pushed out by mass-production and mechanisation.

Evidence from Wainwright's books suggests that he was influenced by the ideas expounded by the founders of the Arts and Crafts movement in the late 19th century as a result of increasing concern about the detrimental effects of industrialisation on manual workers and the quality of manufactured goods.

Like William Morris, Wainwright admired, in particular, medieval design and craftsmanship. He eschewed modern methods of production which, he thought, had abandoned the promotion of craft skills in favour of ease and speed of production, with design and manufacture concentrating on utility rather than on more aesthetic qualities such as simplicity, beauty and pride in a job well done. This approach, he argued, had led to a fall in standards more generally during the twentieth century.

* * * * * * *

Whilst many of his peers became manual labourers in the factories and mills of Blackburn, Wainwright decided at a young age that he would choose a different path. He had greater ambitions and wrote about his future in a school essay: 'When I grow older, I fully intend to apply for a situation in an architect's office, or failing that, a position as office-boy in any other office.'[1] His handwriting was immaculate and he had shown an aptitude for drawing.

On leaving school at the age of thirteen he applied for a position at Blackburn Town Hall, transferring after three years to the Treasurer's Department. He spent years studying for the required examinations in accountancy but it was the practical elements of his training that he remembered, becoming a master of pen and ink:

> 'Accountancy was my line. I was a pen-and-ink man. I was trained to believe that accountancy is an art, and it seemed to my juvenile reasoning in those far-off days that accountants must therefore be artists. I remember being told that every page of my ledgers should be fit for framing.'[2]

He was a true craftsman and was meticulous about maintaining high standards in his own work and, by setting an example, that of his work colleagues:

> 'I enjoyed accountancy. I liked working with figures and proving them accurate by finding them all in balance at year end. There was satisfaction in preparing annual accounts that I knew to be absolutely correct in every detail. I had been taught at primary school to write legibly and keep my exercise books tidy, lessons I never forgot, and it was a fetish of mine, almost an obsession, to keep my ledgers neat, columns of figures being in strict alignment and written narratives as clear to read as typeset print. I took a great pride in my account books and conducted by example a personal rebellion against sloppy work, a prime cause of mistakes and wasted time.'[3]

It is not surprising that when he began writing the Pictorial Guides, he had the same approach to his work, although he had to accept that nothing in life could ever be perfect:

> 'I started the book determined that everything in it should be perfect, with the consequence that I spent the first six months filling wastepaper baskets. Only then did I accept what I should have known and acknowledged from the start – that nothing created by man is perfect, or can hope to be; and having thus consoled and cheered my hurt conceit I got along like a house on fire.'[4]

True Craftsmen

When Wainwright began his series of Lakeland Sketchbooks, he made the argument that his books reached back into the nineteenth century to the days when romantic landscape paintings of the Lake District were fashionable. He wrote, in the introduction to the first volume, that his book was a one-man protest at the decline of artistic and architectural standards during the past hundred or more years. His drawings exhibited his artistic prowess with pen and ink as well as showcasing what he considered the high point of architectural and vernacular design of the buildings and other structures he found in the landscape. He asked, where were the masons who could design and build such beautiful cathedrals, such as York Minster or the craftsmen who built such elegant stone bridges? He pondered whether he had been born in the wrong century:

> '... this book is a feeble protest, one man's private rebellion, at the decline in standards of much of the artistic expression over the past century or more and the present acceptance as art of poverty-stricken and barren inspiration and rank bad execution. Where today is the man who could design York Minster and where is the man who could build it? Where today are the great poets and painters, the composers and sculptors whose works live on in undiminished splendour from one generation to the next? Where today are the men who can build lovely bridges and graceful arches, poetry in stone, such as were built before the age of technology withered artistic enterprise and initiative? ...
> Perhaps I myself am a throwback to the last century!'[5]

Wainwright's sketchbooks and guidebooks were full of examples of vernacular buildings such as cairns, walls, sheepfolds, packhorse bridges, farmhouses, cottages and churches, each one exquisitely rendered and located in its natural setting within the landscape.

He was fulsome in his praise of the common man such as those who built the dry-stone walls in the Lake District. They were anonymous labourers whose monuments had outlived them, but Wainwright wished to honour their memory. The dedication in *The Far Eastern Fells*, reads:

> 'BOOK TWO is dedicated to the memory of
> THE MEN WHO BUILT THE STONE WALLS,
> which have endured the storms of centuries and remain to this day as monuments to enterprise perseverance and hard work'[6]

A Newt in Hard Tarn

It was not just the quality of the structures that he wanted to celebrate, it was the human qualities such as perseverance and hard work, which were inherently part of the design and construction. An example of this can be appreciated in the stone walls on Fairfield, where Wainwright noted that even on steep ground, the stone courses remained horizontal and wrote, admiringly: 'Witness here a dying art!'[7]

The stone wall on the south ridge of High Pike
The Eastern Fells, High Pike, p. 4

'A traveller along the ridge cannot help but notice the wall: it accompanies him all the way and its intimacy becomes a nuisance. However, it is well worthy of notice, particularly on the steepest rises south of the summit, where the method and style of construction, in persevering horizontal courses despite the difficulties of the ground, compel admiration: it should be remembered, too, that all the stone had to be found on the fell and cut to shape on the site. Witness here a dying art!'[8]

Lakeland is dotted with the ruins of former sheepfolds, but none are more impressive than the circular sheepfolds of Skiddaw Forest. Wainwright was in reflective mood when he compared the skill and sense of pride of the unknown man who built them with workers in modern contemporary life, having higher standards of living and better access to education:

> 'In these decadent years of easy money and overmuch leisure, of easy consciences and slipshod work, it is refreshing to come across craftsmanship of the highest standard and be reminded of the days when even the humblest servant took a pride in his work and when hands were the most skilled of all tools.
>
> Such a man, a common hireling, built the circular dry-stone sheepfolds, six in number, that are a unique feature of Skiddaw Forest. (Elsewhere in the district rectangular shapes are favoured).

They are all within easy reach of Skiddaw House and within the forest fence. All are built to the same sturdy pattern, and although probably over a century old have hardly a stone out of place even today. These sheepfolds are *beautiful*, works of art.

The man who built them lived a hard life, working for a few pence a day, having to collect the stones he needed from the fellside and often sleeping rough on the job at nights. He did the task he was hired to do, and did it well. When, in due course, he passed away from this life he left no name behind him. Only his work remains. Just an unknown labourer . . . . but how many of us today, with far greater opportunities and education, will be remembered by our work hundreds of years after we are gone? Few indeed! Idleness builds no monuments.'[9]

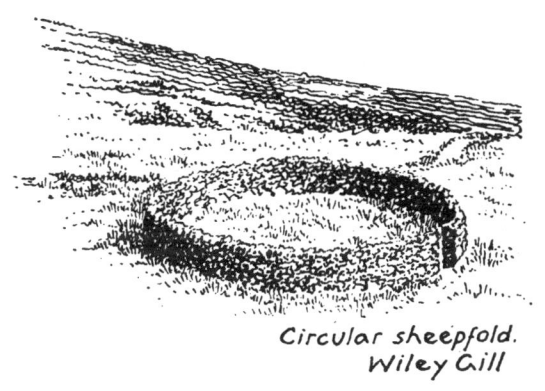

Circular sheepfold, Wiley Gill
The Northern Fells, Great Calva, p. 4

When Wainwright compared building standards of the past and present, he was rarely impressed with modern bridges built of steel and concrete compared with the stonework of much earlier times. His explorations of the western fells of Lakeland took him to Matty Benn's Bridge, an ancient packhorse bridge across the River Calder. It was a simple structure with no parapet, yet had stood the test of time and winter storms for centuries, unlike some modern footbridges that had collapsed:

'The golden age of building passed away with technical advances in the industry, and the craftsmen died when the machines came. Once men built to last; now they build for the temporary requirements of a changing world.

Matty Benn's Bridge was built hundreds of years ago by men who worked with their hands and is still there, a joy to behold, and functional. But modern footbridges put across these western rivers too often perish with the storms.

The tragedy of our age is that we are not ashamed.'[10]

Matty Benn's Bridge
A Third Lakeland Sketchbook, No. 193

Wainwright loved and respected summit cairns. They were old friends, always looked for eagerly after the long ascent. Some were well-known and of great antiquity. Robinson's Cairn on the High Level Traverse route to Pillar Rock, commemorated the life of rock climber and fellwalker, John Wilson Robinson. Westmorland Cairn was erected in 1876 by the Westmorland brothers. In their opinion it marked the finest mountain viewpoint in Lakeland.

The cairn on the summit of Pike o' Blisco was considered by Wainwright to be a work of art and his drawing of it in *The Southern Fells*, was the last view of the original as it was destroyed by vandals shortly before publication of the book. Wainwright issued an appeal for walkers to rebuild the cairn and willing hands completed the task:

True Craftsmen

'Pike o' Blisco has little claim to distinction of outline but seen from The Band on Bowfell, as here, assumes the shape of a graceful pyramid; it also once had a graceful summit cairn, a work of art. It was here that I first had evidence that the vandals of the towns had arrived on the mountain tops. The cairn, having withstood the storms of centuries, I found wantonly destroyed. An appeal for volunteers to restore it found a ready response although the efforts of amateurs lacked the professional skill of the forgotten dalesman who built the original.'[11]

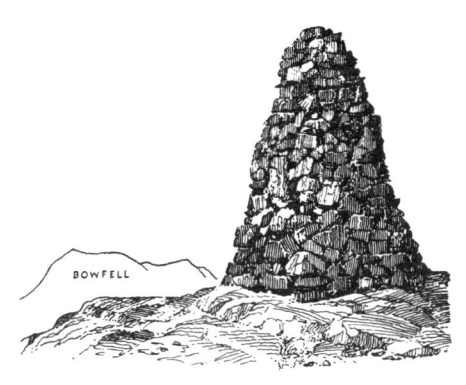

The original summit cairn on Pike o' Blisco (pre-1959)
The Southern Fells,
Pike o' Blisco, p. 9

Another cairn that was admired by Wainwright for its craftsmanship was the shelter-cairn of Josse Pike, named after the gamekeeper who built the cairn in the 1870s. Sadly, this fine edifice was damaged by trespassers in 1974:

The shelter-cairn
Westmorland Heritage, p. 32

'This splendid shelter-cairn, 12 feet high, within the wall of the Barbon Manor Estate, is known as Josse Pike after the gamekeeper (Joseph Parrington) who built it in the 1870's as a place from which he could watch the grouse moor on Barbon High Fell, as a shelter for himself and on top of which a poll-trap could be set for birds of prey; today it is a monument to craftsmanship.'[12]

Perhaps more than any other era in history, Wainwright appreciated the skill and craftsmanship of the medieval period. It was the skill of the masons working with stone using simple hand tools that gave him the most pleasure. He had a particular eye for the ruined monasteries and abbeys such as Shap Abbey, not only praising the skill of the builders but also their sense of location. They were fine buildings that complemented their landscape setting:

Shap Abbey
A Lakeland Sketchbook, No. 76

'The builders of England's ancient country abbeys were not only experts in a craft now either extinct or dormant but landscape artists too: they certainly had a good eye for the most-favoured and pleasantest rural locations. Quiet retreats in sequestered valleys, amidst trees and with a river nearby: these were the requisites and it is small wonder that, in such peaceful surroundings, the buildings too had grace and dignity and beauty.'[13]

True Craftsmen

As well as the great abbeys and cathedrals of the land, Wainwright admired small country parish churches. The church at Ulpha was commended for the craftsmanship of its internal fabric and its perfect location in the Duddon Valley:

Ulpha Church
A Second Furness Sketchbook, No. 59

'Ulpha Church in the Duddon Valley has a history going back so far in time that its origins are obscure, the first written mention of it being in 1577. The interior contains splendid examples of local craftsmanship, and the neat whitewashed exterior blends well into its setting of woodland and fell.'[14]

Wainwright believed that craftsmanship was far more than inspiring design, the use of natural materials and good workmanship together with an innate affinity with the living landscape. It was a state of mind that affected one's character traits and attitudes to work. For Wainwright, actions spoke louder than words and how a task was completed, the care that was taken and the standard of the finished work spoke volumes about character and commitment.

In the 1930s, he had detected a fall in standards that had much to do with the changing world of mass-production where workers were just a small cog in the assembly line, no longer having to take responsibility for the finished article. And these attitudes were spreading to affect other areas of daily life. We had lost the love for a job well done. Wainwright summed up his views in *A Pennine Journey*:

> 'Slip-shod workmanship is a curse; I suppose it is the inevitable consequence of the evolution from individual craft to mass production. The solitary artisan of a century ago was paid according to the results of his labours; the better his work, the more he profited, and if quality was lacking he had to improve or starve. Methods have changed; a man is paid a fixed wage, not for his output, but for the time he spends on it. He has lost touch with the ultimate buyer; his contact is only with the crowd he works with. If he is disposed to slack, or do his work shoddily, only his mates know. There may be others in the group with the same attitude to their tasks, muddling through anyhow, simply not interested, secure in the knowledge that they will not be betrayed. Their inefficiency becomes a strain on the conscientious fellows who have to work all the more industriously to cloak the defects of the idlers. If ever I have aspired to a position of responsibility, it has always been when sloppy, inaccurate work has come to my notice; then, I have thought, how I would like to fork out the malingerers, roots and all, as one weeds a garden. The trouble is, of course, that we have not the same pride in our work that the old craftsmen had. We never dwell lovingly over the finishing touches; often we haven't the time. We never sit back and leisurely contemplate the completed task. We do not love our work the same, nowadays.'[15]

Whatever disappointments Wainwright found in the modern world, he only had to walk in the valleys and climb the hills to realise that Nature was the master craftsman of the landscape, a supreme creator that no works of man could match. The view south from Skiddaw Little Man was near to perfection and brought into sharp relief the contrast between 'nature's quiet artistry'[16] and the works of man:

> 'From this viewpoint, as the onlooker turns his gaze through the southern arc, the picture unfolds like the canvas of a master. This is Cinemascope *in excelsis*, on a scale never envisaged by Hollywood, a vast scene on a screen as wide as the heavens. And all of it is beautiful, nature's quiet artistry. Men are clever enough to make atomic bombs, and strut about like lords of creation, yet they can't even make a blade of grass or a sprig of heather, let alone build up a landscape like this. Which is as well.'[17]

South from Skiddaw Little Man
A Fifth Lakeland Sketchbook, No. 373

However, Wainwright was not against all modern developments. He wrote in praise of the re-routed A9 in Scotland calling it: 'a triumph of planning and engineering'.[18] The new road, a dual carriageway, enabled him to enjoy the lovely scenery on both sides of the road, something that, hitherto, he had been unable to do:

> 'The A.9 merits a paragraph to itself. This is the main road artery to the north of Scotland and is very familiar to the many

like myself whose regular tours of Scotland are the highlights of every year. In the past two decades, the road has been transformed by re-construction and re-alignment into a wide modern highway; every inch of the 114 miles from Perth to Inverness is brand new. Formerly, the A.9 passed through every one of the dozen towns and villages en route but now all are bypassed and connected by offshoots. Formerly there were hazards: snow on the Drumochter Pass, congestion in the village streets, heavy lorries impeding progress. Now there may still be snow at Drumochter – although its passage has been eased by a double carriageway – but all other difficulties have been smoothed away. Once there were 30-m.p.h. speed limits in all the built-up areas; today there are none, and amazingly there is not a single roadside building on the 114 miles from Perth to Inverness. The new road is a triumph of planning and engineering, splendidly graded, and a constant speed can be maintained throughout its length. The journey has become so free of impediments that there is more opportunity to appraise the wonderful scenery on all sides. After travelling on the old road for many years, I have found the changes that have taken place almost unbelievable and, although generally in favour of leaving things as they are, I must admit that the new A.9 is a major improvement and a great tribute to the men who planned and made it.'[19]

Wainwright was concerned that ancient structures such as packhorse bridges should not be allowed to decay once they were no longer serviceable. Fine examples of bygone craftsmanship should be preserved by a responsible organisation for future generations to enjoy. It was good to learn that the old packhorse bridge crossing the River Ribble at Stainforth was now in the care of the National Trust. He was convinced there were lessons to learn from the craftsmen of the past:

'The elegant arch of Stainforth Bridge has spanned the Ribble for three centuries, originally serving the packhorse traffic on an old highway linking Lancaster and York. New routes, modern roads and heavy vehicles have made the bridge redundant, but, as a possession of the National Trust, it remains as a graceful ornament of mellowed stone in perfect harmony with its sylvan surroundings, a reminder of days past when humble men had an eye for beauty and a pride in creating it, an enduring tribute to craftsmanship and good taste. . . . . . The bad old days, some folk call them.'[20]

Stainforth Bridge
Walks in Limestone Country, Walk 29, p. 3

It was not just concern for the built environment that Wainwright championed in his books. He worried about threats to the landscape caused, primarily, through inappropriate decisions being made by official bodies that appeared, to him, to have very little scrutiny by the public of the negative effects this had on the environment. This issue was to be one focus of his writing in his later years.

NOTES

[1] Hunter Davies, *Wainwright The Biography*, p. 20
The manuscript is housed in the Kendal Archive Centre:
Ref: *WDAW/10/1/1/1 School examination paper, English Grammar and composition: My Future*

[2] *Fellwanderer*, unpaginated

[3] *Ex-Fellwanderer*, unpaginated

[4] *The Eastern Fells*, Some Personal Notes in conclusion

[5] *A Lakeland Sketchbook*, Introduction

[6] *The Far Eastern Fells*, Book Dedication

[7] *The Eastern Fells*, High Pike p. 4

[8] *The Eastern Fells*, High Pike p. 4

[9] *The Northern Fells*, Great Calva p. 3

[10] *The Western Fells*, Lank Rigg p. 3
[11] *Fellwalking with a Camera*, unpaginated
[12] *Westmorland Heritage (Popular Edition)*, p. 32
[13] *A Coast to Coast Walk*, p. 56
[14] *A Second Furness Sketchbook*, No. 59
[15] *A Pennine Journey*, p. 120
[16] *The Northern Fells*, Skiddaw Little Man p. 13
[17] *The Northern Fells*, Skiddaw Little Man p. 13
[18] *Wainwright in Scotland*, p. 177
[19] *Wainwright in Scotland*, p. 177
[20] *Walks in Limestone Country*, Walk 29 p. 2

CHAPTER TEN

Conservationist

Wainwright was concerned about rulings made by local and national government and other official bodies that affected land use on upland landscapes and the communities that lived there, and used his books to highlight what he considered to be the harmful effects of poor decision-making. He also believed that cultural assets such as historic buildings should be protected as they added aesthetic value that gave a town or village its unique character and atmosphere.

Although he was not an activist for the cause of conservation, not joining protest groups or organising petitions, he spent nearly forty years highlighting issues that mattered to him where he felt that the authorities had fallen short in their care of the landscape. He suggested the re-use of old buildings instead of demolition and praised examples he found where this was happening successfully. He urged the preservation of fine examples of structures such as packhorse bridges, street furniture and heritage railways. In particular, he emphasised the need for personal responsibility in caring for upland landscapes by walkers and other visitors.

* * * * * * *

It was during Wainwright's first visits to the Lake District, in the 1930s, that he encountered the damage he believed was being wrought on the landscape by two public bodies in particular: Manchester Corporation and the Forestry Commission.

In the 1890s, Manchester Corporation acquired the right to abstract water from Thirlmere, turning it into the first man-made reservoir in the Lake District. When Wainwright visited Mardale in the early 1930s, work was already underway to build a reservoir in that valley. The result was Haweswater, an act of destruction that he could never quite forgive. He had an emotional attachment to Mardale having seen it before the waters flooded the valley.

In *The Far Eastern Fells*, he wrote with sorrow:

> 'Mardale is still a noble valley. But man works with such clumsy hands! Gone for ever are the quiet wooded bays and shingly shores that Nature had fashioned so sweetly in the Haweswater of old; how aggressively ugly is the tidemark of the new Haweswater!'[1]

Haweswater, from the third cairn
The Far Eastern Fells, Harter Fell, p. 10

By the 1970s, responsibility for water supply had been consolidated into ten regional authorities. There was a proposal to create a new reservoir by flooding the Westmorland Borrowdale valley, to which Wainwright objected. In 1972, he included the valley in his book, *Walks on the Howgill Fells*, depicting a route along the Whinfell ridge lying to the south-west of the valley of Borrowdale. The complete ridge walk included a return along the valley, described by Wainwright as: 'a delightful journey even in rain'.[2]

Borrowdale, from Castle Fell
Westmorland Heritage, p. 464

He was so appalled by the idea and, imagining it might be quietly slipped through the planning process without much opposition, he decided to bring it to the attention of the public in his book:

'The threat to Borrowdale
With all the usual hamfistedness of bureaucracy, the Water Resources Board selected Conservation Year[3] to threaten the drowning of more northern valleys. Among them, Borrowdale 'is deemed suitable for a reservoir'. It is probably hoped that there would be little opposition: after all, only a handful of folk make a living there, and although it is the most beautiful valley in Westmorland outside the Lake District this is not generally known and it has few visitors.

But do the water authorities really have to be so cannibalistic? *Must* they devour and destroy *for ever* areas of natural beauty that have taken ages to fashion? *Must* the sacrifice always be the homes of farmers, the pastures of animals, and plants and trees? Take the surplus water and be welcome to it, but can't it be done in a civilised way? Is it beyond the wit of their engineers to devise a scheme for taking water through underground pipes from inconspicuous intakes along the stream bed without the need and immense cost of constructing reservoirs? Well, is it?

Sooner or later the authorities will have to treat and use sea water. Why delay until more damage has been done to our heritage? Why don't they practice conservation as well as preach it? Lovely Borrowdale! Poor poor Borrowdale ...'[4]

The threat to Borrowdale was still there when he published *A Lune Sketchbook* in 1980 and he dedicated it to the Borrow Beck Action Group who were still campaigning against the proposal:[5]

> '*Dedicated to*
> THE BORROW BECK ACTION GROUP,
> formed to oppose the construction
> of a dam in Borrowdale and the
> flooding of this lovely valley.
> *May their cause succeed!*'[6]

Another Government agency that Wainwright had harsh words for was the Forestry Commission. As with Mardale, Wainwright could remember the Ennerdale valley before the trees that were planted after the First World War had grown up to choke the flanks of Pillar. It was not only the desecration of a beautiful valley that angered him, but also the unnatural way that trees were being grown for commercial purposes that caused upset:

> 'Where there are now forest roads in Ennerdale there was once a solitary shepherd's track; where there are now plantations of conifers there used to be fellsides open to the sky, singing birds and grazing sheep: it was Herdwick country, Cumberland at its best. Those of us old enough to remember the valley as it was are saddened by the transformation. Lovers of trees paradoxically will not like the hundreds of thousands that make up Ennerdale Forest: deformed, crowded in a battery, denied light and air and natural growth. Trees ought to be objects of admiration, not pity.

Trees have life, but thank goodness they have no feelings, else here would be cruelty on a mammoth scale.'[7]

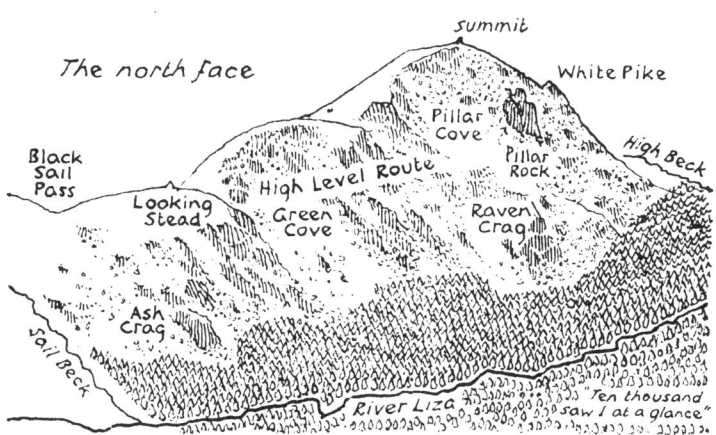

Pillar, the north face
The Western Fells, Pillar, p. 3

In *The Western Fells*, he included a sketch of the north face of Pillar and with heavy irony he had included this caption: 'Ten thousand saw I at a glance'. It was a line from Wordsworth's, *I Wandered Lonely [as a Cloud]*, the poem that exalts the delicate beauty of the wild daffodils on the shores of Ullswater:

> 'I wandered lonely as a cloud
> That floats on high o'er Vales and Hills,
> When all at once I saw a crowd,
> A host, of golden Daffodils;
> Beside the Lake, beneath the trees,
> Fluttering and dancing in the breeze.
>
> Continuous as the stars that shine
> And twinkle on the milky way,
> They stretched in never-ending line
> Along the margin of a bay:
> Ten thousand saw I at a glance,
> Tossing their heads in sprightly dance.'[8]

A Newt in Hard Tarn

Despite his many criticisms of Manchester Corporation and the Forestry Commission, he mellowed in his opinions as the years passed. In his last book, *Wainwright in the Valleys of Lakeland*, he wrote a final conciliatory conclusion to the work that both had undertaken at Thirlmere:

> 'Manchester Corporation and the Forestry Commission have been the greatest predators in Lakeland over the past century. They were not welcome intruders, both being strongly opposed by conservationists and lovers of the district. They have done much to destroy the original character of the scenery and done little to enhance its natural charm. Enough has been more than enough. But it must be conceded that a hundred years of maturity have added a new attractiveness to the Thirlmere valley, best appreciated when viewed from a distance. In the case of Thirlmere, all is forgiven.'[9]

A frequent complaint was the siting of communications equipment on the summits of hills. Wainwright thought that mountain tops deserved dignity and respect. Great Dun Fell lies on the route of the Pennine Way, and he made his displeasure known in his commentary on this section of the route:

> 'The summit of Great Dun Fell is unique. Happily there is no other so defaced, so debased. A monstrous miscellany of paraphernalia, most conspicuous being four tall masts, disgraces it. Additionally there are wind and sunshine recorders, other grotesque contraptions and several squat buildings of no charm whatsoever. . . . A cairn and a few sheep are all one expects, or wants to see, on a mountain top.'[10]

He was even more scathing in his criticism of the G.P.O. Radio Repeater Station sited near the summit of Whinfell Beacon:

> 'When this apparition bursts upon the vision at close range, one's instinct is to flee the place, screaming. But the contraption is NOT a nuclear missile or a spaceship from Mars. It is a G.P.O. radio repeater station, unmanned, used for boosting messages over the hills. It first appeared on the Whinfell skyline unheralded and

unsung, a few years ago. One can applaud fervently the desire to restore 1840 standards to postal services, but what a price to have to pay! A monstrosity like this should never have been allowed to disgrace Whinfell. Was planning permission necessary? Was it sought? Was it granted? Or can a national authority do as it pleases with the nation's landscape?'[11]

The G.P.O. Radio Repeater Station
Walks on the Howgill Fells, The Whinfell Ridge, Walk 4, p. 3

In the Lake District he disliked the proliferation of car parks and caravan sites. In one case, he sent a letter of objection from Mr Dougherty, one of his many fans, to the Friends of the Lake District:

'. . . your love of Lakeland is obvious, shining like a beacon in every sentence you write and never more in evidence than in your references to caravan sites. Of course I agree absolutely. These ghastly eyesores are authorised by people who would recoil with horror if somebody slashed a Constable landscape. I think myself that they should be prohibited in any area of natural beauty. Individual protests are unavailing, and the only hope lies in organised objections by the associations who care for rural England. I have sent the appendix to your letter to the Secretary of the Friends of the Lake District, who shares our views most strongly and has often appeared as an objector on behalf of his association when applications for the development of caravan sites are under consideration.'[12]

Wainwright was at his most vociferous in challenging inappropriate development on the hills and moors, in his *Pennine Way Companion*. On this walk along the spine of the Pennines, he witnessed huge tracts of open moorland being used indiscriminately for, what he regarded as, official acts of environmental vandalism that inflicted great damage to this precious landscape. It was Big Brother at his worst.

In one of his most powerful and eloquent arguments against the excesses of Officialdom, he wrote:

> 'I want to give support to a cause that Harry Appleyard, like a prophet in the wilderness, has been pleading for years. Along the Pennine Way, even in the most unlikely places, one notes with concern the grabbing of open land by a growing number of Government Departments and nationalised undertakings and other bureaucratic bodies. Quite vast areas are sealed off, and access is barred, on the pretext that the land is waste and of little value anyway. Sheep and walkers, who formerly had freedom to roam, are being confined and channelled within permitted areas, and being prohibited, under threats and penalties, from doing (a) this, (b) that and (c) the other. Ancient privileges are being filched. On the Pennines wide tracts of country are commandeered by the Air Ministry and the War Ministry; once-open uplands have become impenetrable forests; lush valleys are being swallowed by reservoirs; even the nature reserves are loud in their prohibitions. Yorkshire folk used to build stone towers on their hilltops, but now all kinds of fancy contraptions in wire enclosures desecrate the skylines. The Pennine Way, in fact, does jolly well to steer a free route through all the prison fences. The former, much-abused private landowners, who at least knew and loved their countryside, were saints compared with the present autocrats who dictate their threats from city offices. The latest area to be sacrificed in the name of progress is near Cow Green in upper Teesdale, where a new reservoir is to drown a district of unique botanical interest despite an eruption of protest. You can't win against Big Brother .... The old landowners did at least wear tweeds and heavy boots, and listened to reason, but you can't argue against these gents in pin stripes and patent shoes. It is a democratic country we live in, friends. This is democracy at work. Sometimes it's hard to believe.'[13]

Conservationist

In many of his books, Wainwright urged that historical structures should be preserved if possible, even if no longer serviceable for the modern world.

In Lazonby, in the Eden Valley, he was anxious that the bridge did not suffer the same fate as Langwathby, where the ancient stone bridge was demolished and replaced by a modern design, constructed in steel that Wainwright called: 'a sad insult to the noble Eden'.[14]

Eden Bridge, Lazonby
An Eden Sketchbook, No. 57

'The road through Lazonby descends to the river, which is crossed by a long and handsome bridge of four irregular arches, named (like others) Eden Bridge. It is narrow by modern standards, but as yet has been spared the fate of Langwathby Bridge. Long may it survive: this is a case where conservation should take precedence over convenience.'[15]

A humble stone road sign caught Wainwright's eye when he was researching *Westmorland Heritage*. This was the book that he wrote to commemorate the passing of the county of Westmorland in the local government reorganisation of 1974. It was important to him that even irreplaceable features such as this road sign should be preserved as a reminder of Westmorland's heritage for future generations:

Hodge Bridge and the stone road sign
Westmorland Heritage, p. 32

'Hodge Bridge, carrying the A.683 over Barbon Beck, is probably 16th century. The stone road sign alongside, of a type not in favour with modern highways engineers, is itself a quaint antiquity, a reminder of days gone by, that should be preserved.'[16]

As well as preserving historical buildings and other infrastructure, Wainwright supported projects that made use of redundant facilities for other purposes. When many railway branch lines closed in the 1960s, some enthusiasts purchased the track and rolling stock and set up heritage railways to encourage tourism opportunities in the countryside. The Worth Valley Railway was one such project that featured in *A Dales Sketchbook*:

'When British Rail closed the branch line from Keighley to Oxenhope along the Worth Valley, a band of railway enthusiasts was formed to acquire rights to preserve the track and operate a voluntary service with steam locomotives and rolling stock and equipment obtained by public subscription. Right well they have done so. If courtesy and cleanliness and enthusiasm are criteria the Worth Valley lads have demonstrated to British Rail the way to run a railway. Everything is maintained in good condition, the service providing a popular attraction deservedly well supported.'[17]

The Worth Valley Railway
A Dales Sketchbook, No. 70

The old corn mill at Chipping in the Bowland area was converted into a restaurant, thus making use of a redundant building that might have been pulled down. The waterwheel was retained as a feature by the new owners. In the same village, another mill had been adapted for use as a chair-making enterprise. Both these imaginative projects resonated with Wainwright and were included in *A Bowland Sketchbook*:

'A former corn mill in Chipping has been most carefully converted to use as a restaurant and the site made ornamental by shrubs and flower gardens and especially by the preservation of the original water wheel, restored to working order and retained as an added attraction, the scene being enhanced by Chipping Brook flowing alongside. Another mill in the village, originally built for cotton spinning, houses a long-established local industry: chairmaking.'[18]

A mill conversion, Chipping
A Bowland Sketchbook, No. 53

And, perhaps surprisingly, second-home owners were praised by Wainwright for the way that they maintained old miners' cottages in the Dales, when they might have otherwise been demolished, thus preserving the historic charm of these settlements:

'Gunnerside, in mid-Swaledale, developed from the intensive lead-mining activity in the lonely hills behind the village, and since the death of the industry at the end of the last century has adjusted itself to agriculture and catering for visitors, while many of the old miners' cottages have been transformed into attractive retirement and holiday homes. The influx of 'off-comers' to the Dales villages is often criticised but where the alternative would be a colony of neglected and decaying properties the 'take over' by outsiders is surely commendable.'[19]

Gunnerside
A Second Dales Sketchbook, No. 97

Wainwright was clear that walkers and other visitors had a personal responsibility to protect and conserve upland landscapes. He considered that part of his role was to educate the readers of his books in practical ways in order that they they could learn how to protect this precious, living landscape.

When writing *The Western Fells*, the final book in his Pictorial Guides series, he decided to give his readers some gentle instructions on the art of good walking:

'There are good walkers and bad walkers, and the difference between them has nothing to do with performances in mileage or speed. The difference lies in the way they put their feet down.

A good walker is a *tidy* walker. He moves quietly, places his feet where his eyes tell him to, on beaten tracks treads firmly, avoids loose stones on steep ground, disturbs nothing. He is, by habit, an improver of paths.

A bad walker is a *clumsy* walker. He moves noisily, disturbs the surface and even the foundations of paths by kicking up loose stones, tramples the verges until they disintegrate into debris. He is, by habit, a maker of bad tracks and a spoiler of good ones.

A good walker's special joy is zigzags, which he follows faithfully. A bad walker's special joy is shortcutting and destroying zigzags.'[20]

The problem was erosion of the footpaths and Wainwright was convinced that this was caused by people not walking in single file. On popular routes such as the ascent of Penyghent the original track was as wide as a road in places:

> '... [Penyghent] is also a compelling attraction for visitors based on Ribblesdale, and the amount of foot traffic so generated has caused severe erosion of the few paths on the soft peat of the upper slopes, the damage being only partially remedied by the placing of duckboards and fencing laid across the path most commonly in use.
>
> When I first climbed Penyghent the path could barely be discerned in the tough grass; today it has the dimensions of a road, its misuse being largely due to parties walking abreast and chattering instead of walking sedately in single file as all should do on narrow paths.'[21]

Litter was a growing problem caused by the popularity of some summits and the natural tendency for walkers to stop for a rest and refreshment. It was not just the litter that looked unsightly, there was also a danger for grazing animals, such as sheep.

Penyghent was a particular magnet for walkers as it was on the route of the Pennine Way as well as being the first objective on the Three Peaks Walk:

> 'Like all popular summits, Penyghent is a dump for litter, some of it (bottles, tins, plastic bags) being dangerous for sheep—which have far more right to enjoy Penyghent than ill-mannered humans.'[22]

Conservationist

Increasing numbers of visitors put pressure on the delicate ecology of the hills. There were many rare plants that were threatened by thoughtless people uprooting them to plant in their own gardens. On the flanks of Ingleborough it was the purple saxifrage that was at risk:

> 'It is here, in crannies of the rocks, that the purple saxifrage may be found in flower in late April, although the display is scanty compared with that on Penyghent's white cliffs.
>
> To take these shy plants is to kill them—they are creatures of the hills; in town gardens they pine and die. So don't.'[23]

The limestone cliffs of Ingleborough
Walks in Limestone Country, Walk 9, p. 4

At the end of the War there was a quickening pace of change in British society. After wartime rationing was brought to an end, living standards began to rise. People had greater disposable incomes and leisure time increased. Car ownership rose and there was an exponential growth in the number of visitors to popular tourist areas such as the Lake District.

There were other changes in the countryside that disturbed Wainwright. The established rural way of life of self-sufficient communities providing local needs was declining. Rural craftsmen were unable to sustain a living and small-scale workshops and factories were closing down or relocating to urban areas. The world that Wainwright had known all his life was disappearing, leaving him unsettled. He felt the need to record a lost way of life before it was consigned to history. Was this merely nostalgia for the past or was there something more fundamental in his mind?

NOTES

[1] *The Far Eastern Fells*, Some Personal Notes in conclusion

[2] *Walks on the Howgill Fells and adjoining fells*, The Whinfell Ridge, Introduction

[3] Europe's Conservation Year, 1970

[4] *Walks on the Howgill Fells and adjoining fells*, The Whinfell Ridge, Walk 1 p. 2

[5] Eventually, the proposal to flood the Borrowdale valley was withdrawn by the North West Water Authority.

[6] *A Lune Sketchbook*, Dedication

[7] *A Coast to Coast Walk*, p. 16

[8] William Wordsworth, *Poems by William Wordsworth, Vol I*, 1815, p. 328 Lines 1-12 Text of *I wandered lonely see* website: https://en.wikisource.org/wiki/Page:Poems_by_William_Wordsworth_(1815)_Volume_1.djvu/388

[9] *Wainwright in the Valleys of Lakeland*, p. 172

[10] *Pennine Way Companion*, p. 57

[11] *Walks on the Howgill Fells and adjoining fells*, The Whinfell Ridge, Walk 4 p. 3

[12] *The Wainwright Letters*, edited by Hunter Davies, p. 250

[13] *Pennine Way Companion*, Author's personal notes in conclusion, pp. xx-xxi

[14] *An Eden Sketchbook*, Introduction, p. vii

[15] *An Eden Sketchbook*, No. 57

[16] *Westmorland Heritage (Popular Edition)*, p. 32

[17] *A Dales Sketchbook*, No. 70

[18] *A Bowland Sketchbook*, No. 53

[19] *A Second Dales Sketchbook*, No. 97

[20] *The Western Fells*, Great Gable p. 16

[21] *Wainwright in the Limestone Dales*, p. 123

[22] *Pennine Way Companion*, p. 110

[23] *Walks in Limestone Country*, Walk 9 p. 4

CHAPTER ELEVEN

Lament for a lost world?

When Wainwright began writing the Pictorial Guides, the pace of change in the Lake District was quickening, and by the early 1960s he was beginning to ask whether the societal changes taking place were beneficial to the landscape and, more widely, to the small communities that lived there. In *The Northern Fells*, he questioned transport policy, the mechanisation of agriculture and, in his own words: 'the march of progress'.[1]

In his later books, he considered more fundamental changes in the countryside; the consequences of the loss of self-sufficient communities, rural crafts and small industry, the growth of car ownership and the development of mass-tourism. Traditional country life and values were disappearing and the old romantic charm of the Lakeland valleys was under threat. Country towns were being redeveloped to accommodate the motor car and the new influx of visitors. But despite the many changes, the hills and mountains remained as they had always been: constant, dependable companions.

****

Uneasy doubts were voiced when he was exploring the approaches to Bakestall in the Dash valley. He was to discover that these northern valleys did not have the drama of those further south. Instead, they had a quiet beauty where rural life continued as it had always done for generations. But even here there were signs that the twentieth century was making its presence felt. Wainwright wondered if the march of progress was taking society in the right direction and whether what was lost from the past had more true value than what was gained:

'Peter House, Mirkholme and Dash are farms. In fact, the scene in the valley of Dash Beck is truly rural. There are no hotels, no private residences, no mansions. All is quiet in this lovely fold of the hills. It seems remote from the busy world, and much more to be preferred. Sheep and cattle graze undisturbed in pastures that tell of good husbandry over the centuries. Sometimes a solitary farmworker can be seen tilling the few ploughed fields, or repairing a wall, or 'doing the rounds' with his dog. Surely this is life as it was meant to be to be lived, close to the good earth? One regret . . . gone from the farms are the fine horses, not the less noble for being servants. Tractors and machines have taken their place. This, we are told, is a sign of the march of progress . . . . but nobody ever tells us where it is marching. It's time we found out. We might be losing more on the way than we are gaining.'[2]

The Dash Valley
The Northern Fells, Great Cockup, p. 4

The end of horse power on the farms signalled the demise of the village blacksmith, no longer needed for his farriery skills. However, the loss of the blacksmith meant that there was nobody to make and mend the farming tools and many other household implements and utensils used by the local community. It was another sign of the decline of country life. Wainwright recorded their passing in the Lake District in *A Lakeland Sketchbook*:

'The Loweswater area is a quiet backwater remote from the main streams of tourist traffic, and still enjoys the tranquillity of the days when motive power was provided by horses. But here as elsewhere, horses have been driven from the roads and the old smithy has closed its doors for ever, to await an inevitable doom.'³

The old smithy, Kirkstile
A Lakeland Sketchbook, No. 9

When he was researching for his book, *Westmorland Heritage*, Wainwright was saddened by the number of villages he visited that had lost many of their craft enterprises and small industries, the ruins of the workshops and mills testifying to their passing. It was these rural industries that were the lifeblood of the villages, allowing the inhabitants to be self-sufficient in their everyday lives. None had been saved as a heritage museum for future generations:

'The decline of rural industries
The most significant change in the countryside over the past century has been the sad decline of rural crafts and industries. Gone are the village blacksmiths, the cobblers, the workers in iron, the wheelwrights. Gone are the hundred little Westmorland mills that stood at the side of streams and, each with its waterwheel, made goods and produce to meet the material needs of the surrounding district. Power was supplied by the wheel, and a handful of workers milled corn or made bobbins or woollens for

local use. Almost all of the rural mills have ceased to operate: some have been converted to other purposes, mainly residential; some stand as gaunt memorials of days gone by, deserted, derelict, ivy covered, with the wheel rotting; some are reduced to a heap of stones amongst rampant weeds. Not one has been saved as a working museum.....'[4]

In the parish of Helsington, lying to the south of Kendal, was the only known working water-powered snuff mill in England. Wainwright was fascinated by the simplicity of its design that allowed it to be the most efficient of machines and he believed that the mill could have a message for the present day. It was completely reliable and used a clean source of power that caused no pollution:

The Snuff Mill
Westmorland Heritage, p. 130

'The water is supplied from the nearby River Kent by a system of races and sluice gates. The wheel never stops its rhythmic movement as long as water is provided. It never complains. It is a most loyal servant. Helsington Mill has never suffered a power strike.

Looking at it one readily begins to doubt the efficacy of the manifold technological inventions, the complex of complicated contraptions with which present-day civilisation is encumbered, that cause so much frustration when anything goes wrong. Here, at Helsington Snuff Mill, is a simple device that never fails, that uses only river water and returns it unpolluted, that costs next to nothing to operate, that produces no fumes or other noxious substance, that generates no heat that would impair the flavour of the finished product, that leaves no litter, makes no noise, and always works perfectly.

It could have a lesson for the 20th century.'[5]

Apart from this isolated case, the watermills of Westmorland had been closed for many years and most rural industrial sites abandoned, victims of social change and economics. Most communities survived, although much changed as local employment opportunities declined.

In the case of Grisedale, a valley situated between the Howgill Fells and the Yorkshire Dales, the story was a tragic one. Wainwright recounted the story in *Walks on the Howgill Fells*. Economic hardship had forced almost all the inhabitants to leave the valley. When Wainwright visited, it was a sad, silent place with little hope of regeneration. It was a classic case study of a rural community left to face impossible odds alone. The valley seemed doomed to be a target for the Forestry Commission or the water authorities, both prospects he viewed with dismay:

> 'Grisedale is an oasis of emerald fields enclosed by dark moors and watered by sparkling streams. On a sunny day in springtime, with the new lambs frisking and the birds singing in ecstasy, the place seems a very heaven, a sanctuary. No traffic. Music but no noise.... Just stillness and peace.
>
> At the turn of the century this pleasant valley was the home of a hardworking and happy farming community. A dozen families lived here, brought up children and worshipped in a tiny chapel.
>
> Today it is a graveyard of ruined farmhouses. Good pastures are turning sour; paths are overgrown..... It has the sadness of death. Hard economic facts have driven life away. Only one farmer still calls it home, but happily others from outside use some of the

pastures as grazing, else all would revert to wilderness. The chapel, its congregation reduced to an average of three, has closed its doors for ever. Even God has been driven out. . . .

Has it a future? As grazing land, yes; but most of the homesteads are decayed beyond redemption. Were it better known, these dwellings might have been saved and restored, but the present clamour for country retreats has come too late to restore Grisedale. The Forestry Commission are moving in. And where the beck plunges down a narrow ravine into Garsdale a small dam could impound a large reservoir; an ominous rain-gauge has already been installed. But surely not. Abandoned it may be, but Grisedale is too beautiful to be drowned. There are too few Grisedales left to delight the eye and offer safe haven to birds and animals and so many wild flowers that flourish best in solitude.'[6]

The ruins of Round Ing
Walks on the Howgill Fells, Walk 29, p. 4

Grisedale was not drowned as Wainwright feared it might be and, returning in the late 1980s, he found signs of a revival in its fortunes:

'Two byroads rise from Garsdale and join to enter the upland side-valley of Grisedale. This is a remote and unfrequented hollow in the hills threaded by a narrow strip of tarmac with the deterrent of many gates. Grisedale once housed a busy farming community but economic necessity after the war caused a sad exodus and the abandonment of farmhouses and buildings. . . . Now some life has returned, those dwellings that did not fall into ruin having been adopted as holiday homes; even the forsaken chapel has been converted into a residence. But Grisedale remains a sad place.'[7]

Lament for a lost world?

The character of rural life was transformed in the years after the War and Wainwright pointed to the motor car as being the principal agent of change. As people became more mobile, the need for local self-sufficiency diminished. With fewer opportunities for employment, local populations began to drift to the towns, while, with increasing prosperity and leisure time, cottages were purchased as second homes or holiday lets by 'off comers':

> 'The social pattern of the rural communities has changed radically in the last generation. Gone is the introspective close-knit fellowship, partly because the motor-car has made the country people far more mobile but largely because of the demand by outsiders for cottages and barns in rural areas for use as weekend and holiday homes, a practice that tends to deprive local agricultural workers of accommodation. To their credit, however, the 'off comers' almost invariably produce commendable conversions and have saved many derelict buildings from decay.'[8]

It was not only in the countryside that changes were felt. In Wainwright's adopted town of Kendal, there was significant redevelopment that Wainwright felt had completely altered the character of the old town, and not for the better. The old 'yards' had been swept away, road layouts were changed, new roads and car parks were built to accommodate the needs of the motor car that Wainwright thought had been given precedence over people. In exasperation, he wrote to his local newspaper:

> 'Dear Sir,
>
> ### THE FUTURE OF KENDAL
>
> Amongst all the clamour for big changes in Kendal now that the by-passes are almost with us, may a small voice be heard?
>
> The clamour is for a radical change of purpose, for modern development and new facilities, for more industry, for greater attractions for visitors, for more car parks – lest the town stagnate. Kendal is a delightful place, paradoxically say those who would change it.
>
> Yes, it is. It is a delightful place because it was not planned, because it grew up anyhow over the centuries without

interference from a surfeit of authorities and developers and consultants and outside advisers.

And why the hurry? Kendal has been here for the best part of a thousand years. Why is the year 1969 so important for decisions about its future? Kendal, even yet, is unique. Destroy the features that make it unique and they are lost for ever. There can be no going back to things as they were if a mistake is made.

Prosperity, the plank of the argument, is not altogether a matter of big turnovers and thronged shops. Prosperity has to do with contentment and tranquillity, too. If stagnation means quieter and safer streets and less noise I am all for it.

Visitors come to Kendal because they like it as it is, not because it has super camping sites and multi-storey car parks and all the fun of the fair. Introduce these things and you introduce a new type of visitor, less discerning and less appreciative.

I, as a resident, like Kendal as it is. I liked it even better twenty years ago before the planners were let loose on it.

I cannot believe that I am the only one out of step.'[9]

Wainwright felt the coming of the motor car most keenly in his beloved Lake District. To accommodate increasing traffic flows, the perimeter roads, such as the A66, were being widened and straightened and he thought that this policy was wrong. He did not want to see speeding motorists in Lakeland that he felt would destroy its old romantic charm.

He believed that Lakeland was for people who appreciated its quiet beauty and wanted to explore the valleys leisurely, climb the mountains and be at one with Nature in peace and tranquillity, not those who destroyed the peace and harmony with their noise and clamour. Perhaps it was the same argument he used against the commercialisation of Kendal; that it would introduce 'a new type of visitor, less discerning and less appreciative'.[10] This piece is from *The Northern Fells*:

'The present road policy in the Lake District, of widening, cutting off corners, easing gradients and generally turning highways into racetracks, is surely wrong. Lakeland, once a sanctuary from noise and fast traffic is being opened up to types of people who wantonly destroy peace and quietness and good order, and are aliens in a place of natural beauty. We should be putting up barriers to keep them out, not facilitating their entry.

Lament for a lost world?

Lakeland is for the folk who live there and appreciative visitors who travel on foot or leisurely on wheels to enjoy the scenery, and the roads should be no better than are needed for local traffic. The fragrant lanes and narrow winding highways add greatly to the charm of the valleys; it is an offence against good taste to sacrifice their character to satisfy speeding motorists and roadside picnickers. Lakeland is unique: it cannot conform to national patterns and modern trends under the guise of improvement (mark the word!) without losing its very soul.

Let's leave it as we found it, as a haven of refuge and rest in a world going mad, as a precious museum piece.

Where are the men of vision in authority?'[11]

In the previous century, William Wordsworth opposed the construction of the Kendal to Windermere Railway in two letters written to the editor of the *Morning Post*.

Among the arguments put forward, he stated that he was not trying to exclude the humbler classes from visiting the Lake District. He felt that the area was already well-served with railway connections but he feared that bringing the railway to Windermere would destroy the peace, tranquillity and beauty of the area.

Not only that, but he had no doubt that an influx of visitors would be seeking entertainment that would lead to unwanted commercialisation of the district. This, he felt, would be morally wrong to expose people to the evils of drink and cheap entertainments, particularly on the Sabbath day:

'Having, I trust, given sufficient reason for the belief that the imperfectly educated classes are not likely to draw much good from rare visits to the Lakes performed in this way, and surely on their own account it is not desirable that the visits should be frequent, let us glance at the mischief which such facilities would certainly produce. The directors of railway companies are always ready to devise or encourage entertainments for tempting the humbler classes to leave their homes. Accordingly, for the profit of the shareholders and that of the lower class of innkeepers, we should have wrestling matches, horse and boat races without number, and pot-houses and beer-shops would keep pace with these excitements and recreations, most of which might too easily be had elsewhere. The injury which would thus be done to morals, both among this influx of strangers and the lower class of inhabitants, is obvious; and, supposing such extraordinary temptations not to be held out, there cannot be a doubt that the Sabbath day in the towns of Bowness and Ambleside, and other parts of the district, would be subject to much additional desecration.'[12]

Wordsworth also made the point that the railway infrastructure and the noise and disturbance it created would destroy the beauty that the visitors had come to experience:

'What can, in truth, be more absurd, than that either rich or poor should be spared the trouble of travelling by the high roads over so short a space, according to their respective means, if the unavoidable consequence must be a great disturbance of the retirement, and in many places a destruction of the beauty of the country, which the parties are come in search of?'[13]

Wainwright put forward a similar argument in his introduction to *Walks on the Howgill Fells*:

'As more and more people flee to the countryside for a brief respite from the towns, the opportunities of quiet rural enjoyment are shrinking. The heavy weekend traffic to Lakeland and the Dales, for instance, destroys the peace that people come to seek.'[14]

Despite his blunt comments in *The Northern Fells*, Wainwright always gave credit to the authorities where it was due. He was pleased that over the years the country lanes were not 'improved' for vehicular traffic by widening and straightening. He was more ambivalent about the proliferation of car parks and caravan sites but he must have realised he was swimming against the tide. He could not hold back the 'march of progress'. Improved transport links and increased car ownership had made Lakeland accessible for the populations of the northern cities and towns and, for many, it was a short drive to enjoy a day out in a beautiful landscape. He was thankful that most day-trippers did not stray far from their vehicles and, for the most part, the fells were unchanged apart from occasional acts of vandalism such as the deliberate destruction of a loved cairn as happened on Pike o' Blisco and Lingmell.

Lament for a lost world?

The Lakeland he had known in the 1930s and '40s was lost in the post-War changes in society, remembered only by those who had witnessed the quieter days of the romantic charm of the valleys and fells. Occasionally, he would share his memories with his regular correspondents. He received letters from Mary Reinbeck for nearly twenty years and often recalled the pre-War years of carefree wandering. This unpublished letter was written in 1986:

> 'Dear Mary,
> It was a great pleasure (becoming rarer) to have a letter from you again and good to know that happy memories are sustaining you in the twilight years. I agree with you that the fellwalking days we enjoyed so much still make life like springtime because of the many recollections we have and we were fortunate to know the Lake District at its most peaceful – before the motorcars came to spoil the valleys. But the tops remain as we knew them and always will. They were good friends weren't they? I wonder if they miss us, too!
> Thanks again for writing to me. Keep well, and keep remembering.'[15]

Wainwright admitted that he did not like change and in his later years he lived in a world of shifting values and attitudes. But the fells were dependable friends, always there when needed. When he could no longer climb the fells, he was content with his memories. He had no regrets when his fellwalking days came to an end.

No, it was not a lament for the end of fellwalking. It was not a lament for a lost world, whatever his reservations. He knew he had more blessings than he could ever count.

Above all, what charmed him was the aching beauty of the Lake District, all Nature's gifts freely given to those who walked in heaven:

> 'This book is not a personal lament for the end of fellwalking and the end of active life, but a thanksgiving for the countless blessings that have been mine in the last eighty years....
> Louis Armstrong used to tell us that this is a wonderful world. He was right. It is. We should all feel privileged to live amid such bounty. We should all be joyously happy. All around us, or within easy reach, are Nature's exquisite pageants in a countryside richly

endowed with delights: gardens of flowers, fragrant meadows, lovely trees where birds sing, chuckling streams winding the tapestries of enchanting valleys below the colourful backcloth of hills. There is beauty everywhere: in the humble daisy, in the dappling of sunlight in woodland glades, in the clouds, everywhere. There are the miracles of renewal, sunset marking the end of a day and dawn heralding the start of another. And the marvels of the changing seasons; springtime bursting into new life after the long sleep of winter, high summer followed by the slow death of autumn. We live in a magical fairyland of subtle charm and it is given to us to enjoy as an absolute gift. You do not need money in your pocket to walk through a field of bluebells or on a heather moor. It is a gift we do little to deserve . . .

Louis was absolutely right. It is a wonderful world. We have more blessings than we could ever count.'[16]

Borrowdale
A Second Lakeland Sketchbook, No. 143

NOTES

1 *The Northern Fells*, Bakestall p. 3
2 *The Northern Fells*, Bakestall p. 3
3 *A Lakeland Sketchbook*, No. 9
4 *Westmorland Heritage (Popular Edition)*, p. 187
5 *Westmorland Heritage (Popular Edition)*, p. 130
6 *Walks on the Howgill Fells and adjoining fells*, Walk 29 p. 4
7 *Wainwright in the Limestone Dales*, p. 28
8 *Westmorland Heritage (Popular Edition)*, p. 39
9 *The Wainwright Letters*, edited by Hunter Davies, p. 245
10 *The Wainwright Letters,* edited by Hunter Davies, p. 245
11 *The Northern Fells*, Blencathra p. 8
12 William Wordsworth, *Two letters reprinted from the Morning Post*, 1845, Letter 1 p. 12 *See* website: https://archive.org/details/ldpd_6412713_000/mode/2up
13 William Wordsworth, *Two letters reprinted from the Morning Post*, 1845, Letter 1 p. 12 *See* website: https://archive.org/details/ldpd_6412713_000/mode/2up
14 *Walks on the Howgill Fells and adjoining fells*, The Howgill Fells, Introduction
15 Letter from Alfred Wainwright to Mary Reinbeck, 16th June 1986 (unpublished)
16 *Ex-Fellwanderer*, unpaginated

Bibliography

Works by A. Wainwright
Unless otherwise stated, all works published by the Westmorland Gazette

Pictorial Guides to the Lakeland Fells
Book One: The Eastern Fells, Henry Marshall, 1955
Book Two: The Far Eastern Fells, Henry Marshall, 1957
Book Three: The Central Fells, Henry Marshall, 1958
Book Four: The Southern Fells, Henry Marshall, 1960
Book Five: The Northern Fells, Henry Marshall, 1962
Book Six: The North Western Fells, 1964
Book Seven: The Western Fells, 1966

Fellwanderer: The Story behind the Guidebooks, 1966
Pennine Way Companion, 1968
A Lakeland Sketchbook, 1969
Walks in Limestone Country, 1970
A Second Lakeland Sketchbook, 1970
A Third Lakeland Sketchbook, 1971
Walks on the Howgill Fells and adjoining fells, 1972
A Fourth Lakeland Sketchbook, 1972
A Coast to Coast Walk, 1973
A Fifth Lakeland Sketchbook, 1973
The Outlying Fells of Lakeland, 1974

Scottish Mountain Drawings
Volume One: The Northern Highlands, 1974
Volume Two: The North-Western Highlands, 1976
Volume Three: The Western Highlands, 1976
Volume Four: The Central Highlands, 1977
Volume Five: The Eastern Highlands, 1978
Volume Six: The Islands, 1979

A Dales Sketchbook, 1976
Kendal in the Nineteenth Century, 1977
A Second Dales Sketchbook, 1978
A Furness Sketchbook, 1978
Walks from Ratty, Ravenglass and Eskdale Railway Co., 1978
A Second Furness Sketchbook, 1979
Three Westmorland Rivers, 1979
A Lune Sketchbook, 1980
A Ribble Sketchbook, 1980
An Eden Sketchbook, 1980

Lakeland Mountain Drawings
Volume One   1980
Volume Two   1981
Volume Three 1982
Volume Four   1983
Volume Five   1984

Welsh Mountain Drawings, 1981
A Bowland Sketchbook, 1981
A North Wales Sketchbook, 1982
A Wyre Sketchbook, 1982
Wainwright in Lakeland, Abbot Hall, 1983
A South Wales Sketchbook, 1983
A Peak District Sketchbook, 1984
Old Roads of Eastern Lakeland, 1985
Ex-Fellwanderer: A Thanksgiving, 1987
Westmorland Heritage (Popular Edition), 1988
Fellwalking with a Camera, 1988

Fellwalking with Wainwright, Michael Joseph, 1984
Wainwright on the Pennine Way, Michael Joseph, 1985
A Pennine Journey, Michael Joseph, 1986
Wainwright's Coast to Coast Walk, Michael Joseph, 1987
Wainwright in Scotland, Michael Joseph, 1988
Wainwright on the Lakeland Mountain Passes, Michael Joseph, 1989
Wainwright in the Limestone Dales, Michael Joseph, 1991
Wainwright's Favourite Lakeland Mountains, Michael Joseph, 1991
Wainwright in the Valleys of Lakeland, Michael Joseph, 1992

Bibliography

Primary sources
1. William Gilpin, *An Essay Upon Prints*, 1768
See website:
https://archive.org/details/essayprints00gilp/page/n19/mode/2up
2. Sir Uvedale Price, *On the Picturesque*, 1794
See website:
https://archive.org/details/siruvedaleprice00pric/page/n7/mode/2up
3. Thomas West, *A Guide to the Lakes*, 1778, Reprint, Forgotten Books, 2018
4. William Wordsworth, *Lyrical Ballads with a Few Other Poems*, J. & A. Arch, 1798
See website: https://en.wikisource.org/wiki/Page:Lyrical_Ballads_(Coleridge).djvu/9
5. Samuel Taylor Coleridge, *Fears in Solitude, written in 1798, during the Alarm of an Invasion, to which are added, France, an Ode; and Frost at Midnight*, J. Johnson, 1798
See website: https://en.wikisource.org/wiki/Page:Fears_in_Solitude_-_Coleridge_(1798).djvu/7
6. William Wordsworth, *The Excursion*, Longman, Hurst, Rees, Orme & Brown, 1814
See website: https://en.wikisource.org/wiki/Page:The_Excursion,_Wordsworth,_1814.djvu/9
7. William Wordsworth, *Poems by William Wordsworth, Vol I*, Longman, Hurst, Rees, Orme & Brown, 1815
See website: https://en.wikisource.org/wiki/Page:Poems_by_William_Wordsworth_(1815)_Volume_1.djvu/9
8. William Wordsworth, *Poems by William Wordsworth, Vol II*, Longman, Hurst, Rees, Orme & Brown, 1815
See website: https://en.wikisource.org/wiki/Page:Poems_by_William_Wordsworth_(1815)_Volume_2.djvu/7
9. William Wordsworth, *Two letters reprinted from the Morning Post*, Printed by R. Branthwaite and Son, Kendal, 1845
See website: https://archive.org/details/ldpd_6412713_000/mode/2up
10. A. Wainwright, *Wainwright's unpublished story manuscript*, 1939, WDAW/1/24/1
MS held at the Kendal Archive Centre
11. A. Wainwright, *School examination paper, English Grammar and composition: My Future*, 1920, WDAW/10/1/1/1
MS held at the Kendal Archive Centre

Unpublished letters
12. *Letter from Alfred Wainwright to Mr Kirby*, 14th April 1966
13. *Letter from Alfred Wainwright to Margaret Ainley*, 15th August 1984
14. *Letter from Weaver Owen to Alfred Wainwright*, 13th June 1986
15. *Letter from Alfred Wainwright to Mary Reinbeck*, 16th June 1986

Television programmes
16. *Wainwright's Highlands & Islands*, BBC Worldwide Ltd., 2003
17. *Wainwright's Coast to Coast Walk*, BBC Worldwide Ltd., 2003

Secondary sources
1. Samuel Taylor Coleridge, *Collected Letters of Samuel Taylor Coleridge, Vol I*, edited by Earl Leslie Griggs, Oxford University Press, 1956
2. Samuel Taylor Coleridge, *Collected Letters of Samuel Taylor Coleridge, Vol II*, edited by Earl Leslie Griggs, Oxford University Press, 1956
3. Samuel Taylor Coleridge, *The Notebooks of Samuel Taylor Coleridge, Vol 1*, edited by Kathleen Coburn, Bollingen Foundation, Pantheon Books, 1957
4. Hunter Davies, *Wainwright The Biography*, Michael Joseph, 1995
5. Richard Holmes, *Coleridge, Early Visions*, Harper Collins, 1998
6. Richard Holmes, *Coleridge, Darker Reflections*, Harper Collins, 1998
7. A. Wainwright, *The Wainwright Letters*, edited by Hunter Davies, Frances Lincoln Ltd, 2011
8. W. Hazlitt, *On Going A Journey*, 1822
See website: https://sites.ualberta.ca/~dmiall/Travel/hazlitt.htm
9. Robert Louis Stevenson, *Walking Tours*: Richard Nordquist ThoughtCo, 11th October 2021,
See website: https://www.thoughtco.com/walking-tours-by-robert-louis-stevenson-1690301

Note: References to books in the chapter end notes are written by A. Wainwright, unless otherwise stated.